Two
Roofs
and
a Snake
on the Door

Other books by the author:
THE STAINLESS STEEL KIMONO
THE GOLDEN TAG
BLACK WINGS HAS MY ANGEL

Two
Roofs
and
a Snake
on the Door

ELLIOTT CHAZE

with illustrations by Jack Davis

The Macmillan Company, New York
Collier-Macmillan Limited, London

About fifteen of the pieces in this book originally appeared in somewhat different form in the pages of the *New York Herald Tribune* and *Life* magazine. The author wishes to thank both publications for allowing him to reprint these revised articles.

The Macmillan Company, New York
Collier-Macmillan Canada, Ltd., Toronto, Ontario

Printed in the United States of America

Library of Congress catalog card number: 63–15279

Designed by Andrew Roberts

DEDICATION

This book is dedicated exclusively to army cooks, dentists, hit-and-run drivers, violin players, bill collectors and the Bureau of Internal Revenue's red-eyed and sincere tax-return examiners. All of them. Everywhere. Wherever they may be.

E. C.

Contents

Foreword

Some years ago in Japan a G.I. friend told me he had cracked the mystery of Japanese writing with his country-outhouse decoding system. He was positive all Japanese writing characters simply were stylized drawings of rural outhouses in various stages of decay and occupancy: "Some a them got a man standing in the door and some got a curly roof or maybe no roof at all—some got two roofs and a snake hanging on the door."

The glaring flaw in his system was that although it established loosely the vulgarity of Japanese writing, he couldn't really read it. At best he could only describe the condition of a particular outhouse as depicted on a given page. The point is, he was so tired of never understanding the Japanese he resolved to do the best he could and the hell with it.

My own inability to cope with the Dagwoodian hungers and crippling raptures of fatherhood and middle-aged maleness has, I suspect, created here a work as sick as the roof-snake solution. In any case I've told the truth. At great pain I've ripped the gloss off American Family Life and laid it bare, exposing it once and for all as the strange guerrilla warfare that it is, unceasing, slippery and exhausting.

There will be those who will say that claiming to have written the truest book on family life is like claiming to be the top miler in a TB sanatorium. A lusterless boast, safe from challenge or comparison. I have no ready answer. In point of fact I have no answer at all.

E. C.

You
Can't
Smoke
in Church

IT IS EASTER SUNDAY AND THE CHILDREN ARE RIPPING at price tags on their new showoff clothing, pausing only to belch coppery belches, boiled-egg belches, and to hammer on the bathroom door beyond which is heard the sound of sloshing as Mary, Jr., bathes her narrow body in the old-fashioned tub. The tub has griffin feet on it and because it is raised clear of the floor it rings like a gong whenever Mary, Jr., drops the long-handled brush.

She drops the brush quite often. Her fingers seem

§ 1 §

nerveless, almost boneless, in the handling of ordinary objects, and do not come into their own except when she is fooling with her hair or zippering or buttoning clothing. The American version of Easter Sunday was invented for people like her, for clothing-people, and she has come home from nurses' training school to dress up with the others and to see all of her dressed-up friends and to accumulate new notions as to how she will dress up in the future.

She has been in the bathroom thirty minutes, which means that the remaining five of us have not been in that very important room during the past half-hour. Chris is weeping at the bathroom door, holding up his new gray pants with one hand and striking the door with the other. He is saying some very bitter things. Any kind of a Sunday is a bad time for him because he does not know yet how to tie his shoes and yet he won't let anyone else do it for him. He always believes he is right on the verge of learning and that any interference will cost him the whole show and set him back to that period during which he simply sat and stared at the laces. The laces are, as usual, not fastened in bows, but you can see that something earnest has been done with the tips of them; perhaps they have been plaited. Half a boiled egg protrudes from his jaws, a smooth bluish bubble. It is not easy to swear around the edges of a boiled egg but he is doing it.

Kim is at the mirror to the left of the bathroom door daubing his pimples with tan lotion. He is dressed in a new mustard-colored suit of lightweight corduroy with fashionable pistol-legged britches that fit like bullfighter pants and show long stretches of yellow sock. I always

§ 2 §

have the feeling he has stepped four inches too deeply into his pants but he says what is the use of wearing socks if nobody can see them? The corduroy suit already looks withered and old. No matter what he puts on he looks as if he has been in a wreck. His new white handkerchief is getting gray. Ever since he stuck it in the jacket pocket the handkerchief has been getting darker and tireder by the minute. "Damn it, Jecca, I'm using this *mirror*," he says. "Can't you see I'm *using* the damned mirror?"

Jecca sighs and moves to the bathroom door. She is wearing an old slip which will not show under her new dress, a navy-blue affair cut and decorated to make her look like a girl-sailor. She hits the door a lick. "Come on out, stupid," she says bleakly. Then she sobs phonily and says: "You get your butt out of that tub and unlock this door, there's other people in the world besides you, Miss Priss!"

"Oh shut up," says Mary, Jr., hollowly from the bathroom. "Quit bucking for an academy award."

Enter my wife in brassiere, patented elastic pants, black suede pumps and a black hat shaped like a bell. Her face is made up to the last eyebrow. She nods at the bathroom door as Mary, Jr., again drops the brush in the tub and you get the impression the black hat has made the donging noise. "Come on," she says to the door. "Come on out of there, think of the others."

Chris has swallowed the egg. His eyes are very red and he clutches his groin. He says without expression, "She is going to make me pee all over this floor."

Sunday.

Easter Sunday.

§ 3 §

Except for the new clothes it is no worse than any other Sunday at our house.

The very day we should be in tune with our Maker we are toilet-minded, time-ridden beasts, growling, grimacing, shoving and running back and forth to the clock in the kitchen to see if we are going to be late for church. It is the only clock in the house and it has a weak and somehow undeclared face so that no matter how many times you look at it you can't remember exactly what it said. There is a hair-thin sweep hand that races around the dial and makes you feel slow and hopeless and beset. Oddly naked and without resource.

Chris used to swallow his collection and we had to start giving him half-dollars instead of nickels because it slowed us down even more than the routine state of anarchy; when he was three it appeared for a time he was going to become a piggy bank. I don't say he couldn't swallow four bits if he was of a mind to; I expect it is just that he is more mature and is beginning to understand that money is where the silver bells and peanut-butter kisses come from.

When we get to church we are in a foul humor, sleepy yet restless. The calm steeple and smooth colors in the windows make me ashamed. I cannot look anyone directly in the eye and my stomach growls during the interval of silent prayer, making oinking noises. I gaze at the yellow pencil which fits in a special socket on the back of the pew ahead. The pencil is for pledging money to the church. I wonder how much the preacher makes and what the air conditioning and the organ cost. Now and then I think of a dirty joke.

Sunday.

§ 4 §

On this particular Easter Sunday after we have taken our family place way over to the left of the sanctuary in the rearmost pew, I am seated between Chris and Kim and I see that Chris's two thumbnails have black-green rims. I don't know what he does with his thumbs. The other fingers are clean and he is drawing a picture of a skeleton head inside a hymnbook. He whimpers when I take away the pencil and restore it to its socket. The inside of the ear next to me is dark amber but the rim is clean. He seems to have more rims than most children and he will fool you in the care of them. Some of them glow. He looks up at me and smiles suddenly. The rims of his nostrils, at this merciful angle, are fine.

We are standing and everyone is singing a hymn I don't know. The tune is depressingly complex and mostly it is carried by the women of the church and it comes out from under two hundred new hats. The feathers tremble in this complex wind and I wonder if all the cinammon rolls will be sold at the bakery before we get there. On this day when I should be shucking off my sins and trying for a new start, I'm dead to the music. The pointed windows rest on their ramps in rows on both sides of the room like rockets ready for launch, stained colors flowing through robes and lambs and rocks. There are a lot of rocks in church glass. But all I really see is a vision of an empty tray in a bakery case where the cinammon buns should have been.

I twist slightly to look at Kim, moving my lips in time to the music so that I give the appearance of singing. He has a fresh haircut of the popular kind, so short in the middle that the scalp shines through. There is a large brown-varnished wood tick in the center of the clearing,

§ 5 §

fastened securely, motionless. Of all the fancy Easter headpieces in the sanctuary this is by all odds the most bizarre. When we have prayed and are seated I tell him about it.

"Cut it out, Daddy." He smiles his honest, outdoor smile.

"I mean it," I say. "You must've got it on the Ordeal." An Ordeal is for members of the Order of the Arrow. They lie under trees in the dark and go hungry.

"Well, get it *off* me." His smile is steady but the skin whitens around it.

I feel in my pockets and find a paper clip and straighten it, thinking to heat the tip of it with a match and touch it to the tick. I secure the folder of matches. You cannot simply grab a tick and pull him off, because his head breaks off in the host and causes an infection. "Come on, get it *off* me," whispers Kim urgently.

We cannot risk an infection because it is too near the brain and yet I am doubtful about striking a match because it occurs to me I've never seen anybody strike a match in church before. Sometimes there are a few candles, but they are lit earlier.

"What are you doing?" My wife leans forward to hiss down the row at me.

"Nothing."

"My God," she hisses, "you can't smoke in here, you know that!"

Mary, Jr., and Jecca stare straight ahead, beautifully dressed, oblivious. Mary, Jr., is radiant in cherry-colored gabardine purchased on the budget plan. There seems to be no other patch of cherry gabardine in the room and she is probably paralyzed with pleasure. There are, how-

§ 6 §

ever, a Godawful number of darkly wrapped girl-sailors like Jecca.

"I'm not going to smoke," I say.

The man in front of me turns around. I know him. He works at the plant where they make concrete pipe. He smiles at me. "Smoke?" he whispers.

"I said I'm not *going* to smoke."

Kim says: "Come on, get it *off* me."

"Put those matches away," says Mary, nodding her bell and trying to look saintly and reproving. There are dozens of other soft black bells in the congregation, but none so active as the bell of St. Mary's. It is written on her face that she wishes she'd known there would be these clusters of other bells. The sermon is finished and the organ strikes up with a growl, seeming to blow waves of Easter perfume against the back of the room where we are. All the feathers and ribbons tremble anew in the powerful current of perfumed music.

When we stand to sing the final hymn before the final prayer the man from the concrete-pipe plant says to me: "It won't be long now, you can smoke in a minute."

I wished he would turn around.

Sunday.

Millionaires
Don't
Go Out
in the Yard

WE LIVE CATERCORNERED ACROSS U.S. 11 FROM A
millionaire and in the twelve years we've been here I've
never seen anyone in his yard. I don't doubt that someone has been in the yard, all I say is they haven't been
in it while I was looking, and I say that millionaires don't
seem to spend as much time in the yard as other people,
assuming that this is a fairly typical millionaire. He is a
gentleman of the first water and you can see him just
about any time you want down at the bank or at the gas
company or even on Main Street, where he is as much at

ease and as friendly and outgoing as anyone. I prefer to think of the yard thing as a mystery so I've never asked him about it. And probably it isn't very mysterious either, since he doesn't have to cut grass and his kids are grown and he never finds it necessary to dash out and tell the telephone man not to disconnect him, to give him a little more time to pay the bill.

This part of U.S. 11 is called West Pine Street because it's in the city limits and has to have a name of some kind. There are eleven children and three dogs and perhaps nineteen cats in our block, which is bounded on the west by a Pontiac automobile agency and a radio station and on the east by a blue U.S. mailbox and a seat to sit on while you wait for the bus.

Most of us in the block are either getting grayheaded or are already gray. There used to be a couple that sat out on the porch in the dusk and argued about which one of them had the last enema, but they are gone. As far as I could figure they ranked enemas the way the Prussians used to feel about dueling scars and it was not only an honor, but also an adventure, to have had the last enema. They had a six-foot-tall colored maid who never missed a day and both the man and woman played an electrical organ which was set up in the living room of their white house. They were by far the most interesting people in the block.

Nowadays there isn't too much to offer in the way of excitement. There is a little boy with jet-black teeth but they are his baby teeth and the larger teeth will be white like anyone else's. Now and then a tomcat eats a kitten and once a gray squirrel fell out of a pine onto his head on the sidewalk, then sat up and beat the hell out of a yellow-headed cat. The squirrel then climbed a tree and I guess is doing all right. These are small things, but in our neighborhood you have to take it as it comes and even with birthdays and graduations the pickings can be thin.

We have a certified public accountant, a seller of insurance, a tourist court official, a couple of widows, a retired clothing salesman and an accident-claims adjuster and a lady who works for a loan company. And a few others. At night most of the lights are out early and very seldom does anyone get drunk, or if they do, they don't get drunk in a way that would be interesting to the neighbors. This, of course, is a shame; but it is what happens to a block when it gets old. There are, however, compensating factors.

Bay, the dog next door, is a compensating factor, even though she is getting old like the block and the rest of us.

She suffers a disease which is destroying the tissue around her eyes and no matter how much medicine they put on it she rubs it off on the grass and is almost blind. But she knows her friends and if she likes you she will go for walks with you and even eat a Hershey in front of the drugstore if you buy her one. She has long lovely hair of a sand color and keeps it licked fluffy. She has great style and when she was younger she was so pretty in the face you wanted to kiss her. For some reason she used to remind me of Lady Ashley in that Hemingway novel about the foreign correspondent who was so cruelly deprived in an airplane accident. Bay is a biter, but I never saw her run out and bite anybody that looked like they were fond of her. She is sensitive to this sort of thing. She has

been operated on and can't have puppies, yet I don't believe this has made her promiscuous. If she is a slut she certainly keeps it a secret and you never see her shivering and yelping and making a fool of herself out in the open like most dogs. I mean even when she was young and could have had any dog in town.

On the days when her face looks especially raw and bad and she comes across the low stone fence to me, I don't know what to do. If I turn away from her I am sick and if I stoop to scratch her I'm sick. Other days her face is better; but always it seems to embarrass her.

The kids all along the block are grown, or are growing up fast, and you see ones that only a flick of time ago were fighting over the swings of the Gym-Dandy set and now they are driving cars and beginning to stalk the opposite sex. The boys get wider and wider up top and the girls grow wider in the bottom and the faces more purposeful, almost stealthy. They can't wait to shake loose from curfew and begin sweating bills and taxes and Blue Cross.

Some are old enough now for marriage and they make me think of when Mary had Mary, Jr., our first baby, and I was kneeling down by the bed, she in labor with hard pains and I said, trying to comfort her: "Honey, don't worry, they'll be after you in a minute, they'll take you on up to the *obituary* room."

As I write this on the porch I wonder how we have managed to survive our stupidity and impatience. There are two new garbage cans out by the curb, silvery, with tops that fit, and next door there is a new can, too. They are remarkably unflinching garbage cans and looking at them you can't accurately imagine the way they will be six months from now. The important thing is that now they are fine, blazing; and beyond them across the street the sun shines on the wall of the millionaire's house.

He has a new can, too.

It must bring itself out and then go back behind the house when it has been emptied.

Flu Manchu

THIS IS THE STORY OF ONE MAN'S LONELY STRUGGLE
against Flu Manchu, an Asian modification of a virus
which swims laughingly through costly seas of penicillin
and mycins.

I'm not dead sure the bug, on this particular occasion,
was an import, but if the idea of a foreign-built virus satisfies the snob in a man, why shouldn't he make the most
of it? During the illness it pleased me to think that down
through the ages the Mongols in their hairy caps, aboard
those shaggy compact ponies, sniffled along the steppes,

cursing the disease, filling the thin blue air with asterisks and obscene stars and worse.

They had no Kleenex or orange juice, those boys, no fifty-cent capsules or Blue Cross plan. When my temperature reached 103½ I saw them very clearly as they straggled across the bedroom wallpaper, heads sweating, pausing now and again to bend from the saddle for a quick snort of snow.

My wife Mary swears that in the third night I talked singsong in my sleep and made giddap noises. She testifies further that I kept clapping my heels into the mattress and laughing in a high-spirited, hoarse and reckless manner.

Her suspicions were confirmed the following morning when I demanded brown rice and milk for breakfast and she informed me without bitterness or sympathy that in the twenty-odd years of our association there hadn't been a grain of anything but white rice in the house. "Furthermore," she said, "your Southern belle grandmother would turn in her grave if she heard of you putting anything but gravy on your rice."

I explained patiently that where the hell was a practicing Mongol going to find any gravy, and him suffering with Asiatic flu a hundred miles from a cooking pot and half out of his head?

She wanted to know where he was going to find any rice. Or milk for that matter.

It seems to me, and I say this without heat, that Mary spent the whole time I was sick splitting hairs over things like that. She finally called the doctor who is a good friend of mine and he, no doubt overburdened with work in the middle of his richest flu season in years, and

crazed with concern over my condition, came out to the house and told me to shut up.

My doctor's name is Theophilus Erskine Ross, which, of course, has nothing to do with him telling me to shut up about the brown rice; but which, in an oblique way, supports the fact he doesn't take any foolishness off anybody.

Not that my request was altogether foolish, because, you see, what I'm trying to get across is you ought to squeeze every drop of glamour you can get out of your dose of flu; and really, the least your friends and relatives can do is play the game. It being a Saturday, the children were home when the doctor came and I hated for them to hear him fussing at me. I try to project a fairly powerful and wise image for them and at times it is not easy. Now Chris, who is six, sticks his head around the door and I smile at him and say, "Hello, old buddy." Chris says without explanation or feeling, staring thoughtfully at me with his mean little blue eyes, "He's my buddy, tried and true, stands behind me 'till my belly's beat blue; and when I run, he runs *too*." I assume it is something he learned at school. He flunked the first grade, getting off to about as bad a start as is possible under the present pattern of formal education, but he must have learned something during those stern lost hours away from the house. He withdraws now from the sick-scene.

"This fella's got quite a fever," Theophilus Erskine Ross says to my wife. "How much does he weigh?"

Mind you, he didn't ask *me* what I weighed. From the moment Mary blabbed that I thought I was an Asian cowboy he began halfway ignoring me, acting as if I didn't know anything about my own bowels or fever or weight.

"Two twenty-five," I said anyway.

"That's right," said Mary.

"Then he can take as many as three aspirin at a time."

"Fine," said Mary. She sounded pleased. There was a tinge of respect in her voice.

"Give him some aspirin now and then, that'll cool him and ease the aching and chase those horses off the ceiling."

"Is this the real Asian flu?" I asked.

"I don't know," he said. "But you're a sick man and probably will be for a week or so." He scribbled a prescription and handed it to Mary. "I didn't know he was that fat," he said.

She studied the prescription as if she could read Rexall as well as English. "Oh yes, he's that fat all right."

"Too bad," said Theophilus. "Really a shame, but we"ll get to that later."

When he was gone I felt fatter than I had in years, which, in point of fact, I was. But I felt easier, too. It's always like that. Once he comes and goes I feel the responsibility has shifted to his tough little shoulders and that if I die, it's no longer my fault, it's his.

"How about some cornflakes?" Mary asked. "Some good old Siberian cornflakskis?"

They weren't bad.

But by midafternoon both the mood and the fever were broken. And after that it might as well have been any kind of flu, any kind at all.

§ 18 §

Re
Uncle Lane
and Metabolism

A SOURCE OF WONDERMENT AND CHRONIC SORROW TO me is the fact that my metabolism is perpetually out of tune with the times.

During the first twenty-eight years of my life I was slender as a sword. But in those days it was considered unfashionable if not dangerous to be thin.

Even now I can hear my Uncle Lane saying to my mother: "The boy needs some *meat* on his bones, he looks peaked."

"Well," she would say, "his daddy was thin, you remember Louis." Then darkly: "It kind of ran in his *family.*"

My uncle, who was fat as a hog, was an oil-drilling type and he drove a plump mud-covered Buick. Invariably the Buick was almost new and filthy and there was something hell-rake in the idea of a fine car treated with such carelessness. He was always talking of making a *man* of me and he spoke of this with such quiet concern and intensity you got the impression my penis was not at all securely attached and might drop off altogether along with other evidences of maleness if I failed to work at manhood each day of my life. He made being a man seem a perilous project at best and it appeared that sheer size had a lot to do with it. In World War I he was a machine-gunner and once I saw a picture of him in uniform, with leggings. I was everlastingly impressed by those great brown spiraling legs.

He had three sisters, two besides my mother, and one or the other of them was generally saying something complimentary about him whenever he stopped in our town, and at times when he wasn't even there. If you offered no comment, and I rarely did, they would jog you with a finger and say: "Now, tell me, isn't Uncle Lane a fine figure of a man?"

Once my Aunt Clara said she certainly hoped I grew up to look like him; but you could tell she figured I never would become so gross and marvelous.

Every summer he would take me off for a week or so and try to fatten me up and make a man of me. We tramped around in the woods surveying drilling locations, inhaling mosquitoes and eating in roadside restaurants where the water tasted of petroleum and the dishes were divided into compartments, one for the mustard greens, another for black-eyed peas, and so on. My uncle cleaned out hundreds of the little compartments, getting larger and more manly every day.

But the fresh air and coarse, abundant supply of food did nothing to enlarge me and my mother was barely able to conceal her disappointment when he brought me home looking scrawny as ever, basic and glum as an X-ray picture.

"He'll fill out," my uncle promised. "Anyway he's *tougher* now than he was." This was vaguely reassuring. If he could take pleasure in my increased toughness at least he didn't plan some day to build a fire in the woods and eat me.

All my friends were "filled out" except one whose name I'm not about to recall here, for it was suspected he was inhabited by parasites. The worst thing you could say about anyone in those times—man, woman or child —was that they looked puny or peaked. If you called somebody skinny it was grounds for a fight. To refer to a mature female as skinny was to say she had no sex appeal and likely would bust wide open with her first baby provided she located a male depraved enough to fertilize her. "Why, man, you'd have to shake the sheets to *find* her." If you described a male as skinny it meant he was a weakling or, at least, inclined in that direction and probably headed for the tuberculosis sanatorium. It didn't matter that he had the courage of a lion, he was to be pitied and stuffed. His family began inquiring discreetly as to the costs involved in adding onto the house a screened "sleeping porch."

After World War II people started talking about diet-

ing and the importance of being trim. The word skinny dropped out of the vocabulary; now it was *trim*. Well sir, what with the K-rations and all I was still trim as a bayonet and, as I recall, I was in vogue perhaps six months.

It took me a year after my discharge from service to pack fifty pounds of meat onto my bones and at 225 I weighed about as much as my uncle did back there when we were stumbling in the woods with the lease hounds. I still do.

Broad and deep in the belly, a face maroon as embers. When I eat fried chicken one expects me to rare back and fling the bones and laugh a great heraldic kind of laugh.

But nowdays it's out of style to be a slob and neither my mother nor her sisters ever refer to me as a fine figure of a man. I was home a few weeks ago and my mother and Aunts Clara and Madeline were telling me about one of the slimming powders you mix with water and swallow instead of eating real food. While we were talking my uncle drove up in a Cadillac without a speck of mud on it. He had lost forty pounds and was lean and fit as a razorback.

"You really ought to get rid of that extra weight," he said. "It's bad on the heart."

I'm Not
Going
to Rub
It
in My Hair

MY BREATH IS AN APRICOT MIST AND THE BLOOD OF ME
churns with health-building minerals.

There can be little doubt that after two days on this
eat-all-you-want type diet my mineral content is such
that any good electromagnet could scoop me up with a
clang.

It all began when a friend, who is flat as a slat, told
me I could eat what I wished and slough off pounds in
the process. He said there was nothing to it, once you
accepted the horror of it.

§ 24 §

The secret, he said, was not how *much* you ate—but *what*. And if you could swallow the *what* you had it knocked. "Eat until you're full," he said, without blinking a lash. "Stuff to your heart's content."

He prepared me a list of low-caloric goodies, protein wafers, nonsugared preserves and jellies, stewed dried fruits. He said his wife used the list to good effect. Him? Why no, he'd never dieted a day in his life; he had a thing about turkey and dressing and giblet gravy and if he didn't get his quota of it he wasn't fit to live with.

That night I soaked a bagful of dried apricots until they were slightly swollen and stewed them until they were a glowing burnt orange color, all the wrinkles going out of them. It may be noted here that both apricots and prunes grow younger and younger on the stove.

I'd bought also a pair of elegant Bartlett pears and a jar of little beets, perfect and radiant as rubies.

"You are going to eat this?" my wife asked.

I tickled the underside of an apricot with the cooking fork, "I'm not going to rub it in my hair." I told her she and the kids could have some of the apricots when they were done. Kim, who is fifteen and an Eagle Scout and who had just arrived from football practice with small new scabs on his cheekbones, peered into the pot. He leaned back and laughed sincerely and honestly, employing what I have come to consider his official Scout guffaw.

My wife fed the children spaghetti and meatballs and she did not return to the kitchen, where now the sweet swirls of fruit steam were tantalizing. I placed a dish, a dinner plate, over the pot (we have but one pot cover; why are there always more pots than pot covers?) and smoked a cigarette until all of it was ready. I opened a can of frozen unsweetened papaya juice and colored it twistingly with streaks of lime.

Next I broiled a sheet of fatless steak and surrounded it on the platter with three pieces of dry, rustling, scientific toast.

I have eaten worse food but never in civilian life. Once I drank some water from a wagon rut in the Philippines and it tasted better than the juice. By the time the apricots were downed the insides of my cheeks felt peroxided.

Next day I skipped breakfast and lunch but by suppertime the bile had settled and again I hit the apricot trail, adding prunes and some of the jeweled beets, which were hard and acid little disappointments. The jar said they were Harvard beets. They were round and had no points on them at all and if the label is accurate it does not speak well for the school.

The morning of the third day I managed three of the freakishly young-looking apricots. They struck my stomach like perfumed iron, along with a few jagged splinters of the joyless toast. As this is written lunch remains a sullen threat on the horizon of a dying appetite. It pains me to consider it and I'm grateful for the four hours remaining.

There is no question but that the diet would work.

You can eat all you want but, and this is the key to the whole mess, you get to where you don't want any of it.

§ 26 §

I'm Not
Going
to Let
It Rain
on My Hamburger

THE DAY WAS CLEAR AND THE TIRES OF THE NEW CAR buzzed importantly against the pavement. The children were silent, caught in the mobile magic of the trip. They like trips. They get a charge out of just going to the grocery store or the hospital. And when we pack up and leave town for vacation their eyes glaze over with happiness.

But after a time they want to start eating and today was no exception. "No," I said, "this is *one* car we're going to keep clean."

§ 27 §

"My stomach hurts," said Mary, Jr., who is twenty-two and not really a child at all and who is studying to be a registered nurse at Charity Hospital in New Orleans and already has seen whole jaws removed and parts of intestines. She delights in describing the colors of various internal organs, the pinks and pale blues and yellows, and no doubt she knows the exact hue of the portion of her now in pain. "It always hurts when I get empty."

I gripped the wheel more tightly.

Because when Mary, Jr., is riding in a car and says a thing like that, it is entirely possible she is not kidding. Once when she was little and we were traveling together without the others she warned me and I ignored her and she vomited all over the inside of a full-sized Chevrolet, obscuring speedometer, gas, oil and temperature gauges. It was a freezing day and I had to pull the car to the curbing in downtown New Orleans and change her clothing on the sidewalk, a sight no doubt bizarre even for residents of that imaginative and sinful city.

So now I stopped and bought hamburgers at a roadside cabin with a giant brown plaster model of a Southern fried chicken on the roof. The man behind the counter, at my request, placed the hamburgers in a double bag so the grease wouldn't come through on the new car seats. And he diapered the wet bottles of coke with paper napkins. After all, you don't make a vacation trip in a new car every summer.

Down the road I pulled off onto the clay shoulder and distributed the sandwiches. I smiled my good sport smile. "Now let's all get out and eat."

"It's raining," my wife said. "I'm not going to let it rain on my hamburger."

§ 28 §

It was barely sprinkling. The children tore at the wrappings of their hamburgers and made no move to climb out. Jecca, who is twelve, and at times almost professionally clever at mutiny, observed: "There aren't any signs to eat by, anyway." The younger children prefer to read advertising signs while chewing hamburgers. They have found that if they chew a single time for each individual letter in a sign it makes the hamburger last much longer, in fact, practically forever if there are enough billboards and similar literature.

I fought for control. "You and Chris stay inside," I told my wife. "The rest of us will get out."

"Kim's got a cough," my wife murmured, then gagged and blanched. "You've given me mayonnaise again."

Sorting hamburgers for this bunch is a nerve-wracking assignment since some members of the family detest mayonnaise, others abhor onions, and still others panic at a trace of pickle. Through the years I have worked out a code with toothpicks stuck in the sandwiches, but there are recurrent days like this one when the system breaks down and I stare blankly at bristling buns and hand them out all wrong.

We managed to get straight on the mayonnaise.

I was cheered and pleased with the way I'd arranged the cokes on the floor, in a solid triangle, like pins in a bowling alley. The pattern had beauty and effected economy of space. Kim kicked the coke at the forward point of the triangle, scoring a strike, all six bottles going down in a brown foaming mess on the unstained carpet.

The older children and I ate in the rain on the side of the road, my wife and Chris, the youngest, staring through the glass at us. Occasionally Chris would stick his head out the window and scream at Kim. "You stole my old testimonial." Chris frequently believes one of the others has stolen something from him, but this was a new angle. "He thinks I took the Old Testament part of his Sunday school Bible," said Kim without bothering to answer Chris. "Someone tore the Bible in two," Jecca said. "I think Chris did it himself last summer and forgot about it, I think he sold it to the little girl down the block for a muddy old dead dragonfly with the tail gone."

In the car again and headed for my mother-in-law's, Kim's cough worsened and a cruel thirst gripped the clan. Kim's voice hasn't finished changing, but his cough has. He coughs like a grown man, sometimes like a bear. Some of the children pushed their heads out the windows and extended their tongues to catch raindrops.

A few miles farther, north of Natchez, I stopped for water and coughdrops.

By the time we reached Alexandria, Louisiana, I felt better about all of it, reasoning that my pettiness and loss of face had been worth the price. Perhaps you think me a miserable wretch for trying to protect the car at the expense of child comfort, but on one occasion I found an ancient mustard pickle behind the front seat of the old car. This pickle was as long as a man's middle finger and it was of a color, texture and odor beyond description, fleshlike and drowned.

Another time, in another car, I found a chocolated almond stuck to the knob of the turn-indicator lever. I have through experience learned to identify the delicate scroll-like smears of the two girls and the bold finger-painting of Chris and Kim. Bill, the other boy, who is now a newspaperman in Oklahoma, used to stand apart from the pack, an artist of the first class whose work was as distinctive and rich in color as any I have seen on a dashboard: the ketchup and chili blended in such a masterly fashion that one could not say with certainty where the one began and the other left off. After he started dating I once discovered lipstick and mustard on the ceiling of a '49 Oldsmobile, a fact which intrigues me to this day, and about which I refuse to ask him lest his explanation fall far short of my imaginings.

When the suitcases were in my mother-in-law's house and I'd raised the gleaming door glasses I switched on the dome light for a last smug look at the upholstery of the new car.

The navy blue cloth was crisscrossed with waxy golden threads. I touched it and smelled it. It was stuck fast and when you pushed a thumbnail under it it popped loose and left a whitish stain. In some manner known only to them and the honeybee the children had broken down the sugars in the coughdrops and converted them. There were waxy etchings on the ceiling, too.

I felt like screaming. There was a single unused coughdrop on the floor and the light winked in its translucent depths, golden and slick.

I popped it in my mouth and climbed in the back of the car, sucking thoughtfully until it was gone. It calmed me, and later, when I went in the house, Mary's mother had made a pot of fresh coffee and she said the new car certainly was a beauty.

After coffee everything was fine; in fact, almost wonderful.

The children were in bed for a nap, even Mary, Jr. They were in my mother-in-law's beds, the ones with the pink embroidered sheets, eating sandwiches of peanut butter and grape jelly.

The Lucky
American

A FEW WEEKS AFTER WE HAVE RETURNED FROM THE visit to my mother-in-law's we are driving to the bus station to pick her up. It is her turn to visit us, but this does not dismay me. She is not a bad type. And it is a fine night and our stomachs are serenely full of pork chops, okra and tomatoes. The car runs nicely and when we stop for a traffic light the colored reflections glitter on the hood, strawberry, lemon and lime. I'm suddenly acutely aware of the creature comforts we enjoy as a family.

I say, "You know, we're a lucky bunch."

§ 32 §

My wife appears startled. Gratitude for the *status quo* is not one of my outstanding traits.

"We've got plenty to eat and a roof over our heads," I persist. "We've got transportation and a steady job, ah, on the days I really *do* sit at the typewriter; and your mother is coming, your mother is still alive."

"I certainly hope so," says my wife, drawing in her breath. Then she sighs. "I'll never eat another pork chop, it makes my tooth hurt."

She has more than one tooth but rarely do we discuss the others. The tooth remains sensitive despite overwhelming advances in the field of dentistry. This rather decent-looking tooth has been X-rayed so many times I am certain it would shatter a Geiger counter.

"Oh well," I say, because there is nothing else to offer. I am reluctant to surrender the idea that we are wonderfully lucky. It is so seldom I feel even slightly lucky I am trying to hang on, to savor it.

"Chris got himself clawed again by the kid down the street," says Jecca, our chronic demolitionist, from the back seat. "He looks like a tiger slapped him." She leans forward to hiss in my ear as we brake to a halt in front of the bus station, "Chris-ss-s is a ter-rible cow-ard."

"He's only *six*."

Jecca knows this disturbs me. I have tried to teach Chris to defend himself. He will punch a pillow with fierce silent speed and at times even will growl at the pillow and show his little teeth, no bigger than seeds, and most of them gone in front because he barely waits for them to loosen before he insists I pull them. They are worth four bits apiece; we put the money under his pillow and tell him the good fairy or the rat, or something, places the four bits there. Anyway he is quite the basher of pillows but when it comes to a real fight he is yellow as butter.

"I'll be seven in December," pipes Chris. He doesn't resent the brand of coward, but he loathes being six.

"He's so loud," says Kim. "I wouldn't mind a *quiet* coward. He never shuts up."

Kim's fifteen-year-old voice is hoarse with fatigue. He is always tired these days, what with football and a fairly heavy study load. Now I ask him how it's going with the football and this is a mistake. "I didn't make the first team," he says.

Jecca fills an embarrassing silence with an old and familiar lament. She says all her friends are taking dancing. No additional comment is necessary. We've been over it many times and she knows her toes must remain untrained until the budget is roomier. "Every single one of them," she says. This means every single one of her friends is enrolled in the school of dance. Jecca is undaunted by Mary, Jr.'s, dancing accident of a decade ago. On a fine October afternoon at dancing school Mary, Jr., slipped and crashed on her tailbone and the teacher phoned me to say, "She won't budge, we can't get her off the floor, sir, she says she won't get up for anybody but you." Which was true. I drove a half-mile to raise her and it was rather like getting a horse up off the ice, only much noisier and to less purpose. It concluded her ballet career, but did nothing to dim Jecca's appetite for that duckfooted form of the arts.

The bus arrives and I steer my mother-in-law Jessie to the car. There is kissing and helloing and polite shrieking and for a time good cheer is restored. But Jessie is

§ *34* §

no sooner settled than she tells me a friend of mine ("He's just your age, honey") dropped dead at the bank in Alexandria, Louisiana. He is standing there waiting to make a deposit and bingo, says Jessie.

"You never know," she says. "You just never know, do you? People dropping like flies all the time."

Kim says tiredly he knows a boy only fourteen who has a silver plate in his head and if he's ever kicked in that plate he will die before the ambulance comes.

I start the car and we head homeward. The same traffic light catches us again. This time I hear a clinking in the engine as we wait. No one says anything and finally I slap the steering wheel and say, "I still think we're a lucky bunch—just *barely* lucky, but lucky."

"What on earth is he talking about?" asks Jessie.

When none of the others answers, she begins relating in detail how my friend looked on the floor of the bank.

As the Hair
Is Cut,
So the Man
Is Bent

ABOUT FOUR HAIRCUTS AGO I STOPPED AT A SPORTING
goods store and bought a punching bag of purple leather.
It seemed quite natural that a fellow with a crewcut
should spend fifteen dollars on a large bag shaped like
a fig.

What I'm getting at is that a new haircut is one of
the gravest gambles a man can take within the framework of everyday routine. For years I was unwilling to
accept the fact I didn't wear the haircuts, that the haircuts wore *me;* that a crewcut made me feel absurdly
athletic whereas a pompadour made me want to wiggle

my knees and sing of hound dogs. And going without a haircut for a few weeks kindles my artistic awareness.

The day I purchased the punching bag I'd got myself a bristly square-sided haircut of the type once favored by Gene Tunney. If I do say so, the bag was and is a good one, with splendidly sewn seams and a nice smell to it. I didn't have the money to buy the circular rebounder from which the bag is supposed to hang like a hornet's nest, so I keep it on the top of the china closet and now and then I take it down to feel or smell it and remark on its hardness.

I contend, naturally, that if I'd not gotten the haircut I wouldn't have wasted the money on the bag, nor would I have been forced into telling a whopper to Kim, who believes I bought the thing for his birthday.

Generally I arranged for milder and less demanding haircuts than the Tunney one, more often than not getting what my barber describes as the businessman's special, neither long nor short, almost insipid.

It is the sanest of all and I find that when my scalp lies in the modest clasp of this haircut, decisions regarding financial matters are more reliable. There is little if any interest in exercise or art.

I'm a hog for art when my hair is long. The bush tickling the tops of my ears does something to me. This kind of hair makes the face appear smaller and more thoughtful and it drives me to buy oddly designed ashtrays, preferably ceramic ones from Italy, painted inside with portraits of raw hamburger patties and onion wheels and cross-eyed girls who sit in a tangle of overlapping colored squares and cubes, squeezing their breasts.

Sensitized to color and form I yearn for a lump of

jade to stroke in the Chinese manner. I would like a slab of lapis lazuli or a bit of alabaster. I am given to darting into jewelry stores and asking to see a black opal, although I learned a dozen years ago there wasn't a black opal in our home town and probably never would be.

Normally I'd as soon stub my toe as sit down to the typewriter, but long hair goads me to Produce—not just ordinary story stuff but broad ringing prose-poetry filled with great trains clanging through the night and oceans sucking at their shores in the tradition of Wolfe, some of it by sheerest accident I'm sure, following whole passages of *Look Homeward, Angel* almost thought for thought, indeed, word for word. I prefer to sell stuff but when the hair is rank and lengthy I'm willing to suffer and strain for the pure reward of seeing the words pop from the ribbon onto the good white paper.

There are, of course, variations of long and short haircuts, each with its distinctive mood, and once for the better part of a fortnight I felt pretty much like a German tank commander. At the time I happened to be a member of the 11th Airborne Division on the island of Luzon, so I didn't say anything about it to anyone.

Long before I reached full growth and responsibility, I once went five weeks without a barber's touch and the result was enrollment in a piano class for beginners. I learned to play two pieces, one of which was entitled "Indians, Indians Everywhere" and the other, "Rowing in the Wind." I can still play "Indians" under certain stimulating circumstances, but my wife Mary laughs.

No matter, you see how it goes, and it is a chilling thing to realize that the very trigger of a man's destiny swings from the shape of the hair on his head.

The Man
with
the Golden
Lungs

I STAND AT THE BEDROOM WINDOW TAKING SNUFFLING breaths of the cool heavy air, eyes pink with coughing. I realize with a degree of horror that it is going to be one of those days when I try to quit smoking.

Whenever I wake up and cough a certain way, it's going to be one of those days. Prior to arrival at the window I have hacked steadily for five minutes, running the scale: strangling-kitten sounds, whoops and broken guitars.

After closing the window I stand there for a time before officially deciding to quit. I like to tease myself

§ 40 §

about it, roll it about in the dark recesses of my nervous system where the twanging skeletons of so many dead resolutions lie grinning and moldering. I don't believe in quitting anything on the spur of the moment and sometimes toy with the idea six or seven minutes, feeling lonely and gallant and nervous.

Now I shape the decision and close the window. This time it will be different. Once I decide I'm finished with cigarettes there is for a time no wavering of resolve.

And the decision brings with it a rich surge of energy and sensitivity which, I contend, transforms me from the dimmest sort of clod into a potential celebrity. I feel fleetingly that talent sprays from every pore and follicle and if I can only channel these radiations, harness them, I can write for the first time in my life something that really satisfies me. Unfortunately, quitting smoking makes me too nervous to write, so the notion has never been put to test.

This morning I've been off cigarettes perhaps ten minutes when, tingling with talent, I observe the window fastening is shaped like an iron chicken gizzard. This, you will admit, is creative thinking.

"Look," I say to Mary, "how this thing is twisted and curved."

She is obliging enough to look at the metal window lock but it does nothing for her and she accepts with reservations the idea of the gizzard. I clap her on the shoulder and say with awful good humor, "I feel *wonderful!*"

She backs away. "Ah, no, not again. I'm not going through it again and neither are the children."

"Through what again?"

§ *41* §

"You've *quit* again, there's a funny look about you."

I smile and shrug, lungs stinging with oxygen, a faint buzzing at the back of my head.

I leave her and go into the bathroom and brush my teeth. Morning sunlight glows in a bottle of Lavoris in the medicine cabinet, a quiet red explosion remindful (under the circumstances) of the Holy Grail. My brain feels so painfully alert it occurs to me I might even be able to understand geometry, a subject that has cowed and persecuted me through the years.

En route to the office I feel exaggeratedly alive, aware of sounds and smells long forgotten. During the walk I slap the rough bark of several trees, enjoying the harsh bite of it. I whistle. I grin to the jaw teeth at a startled fellow walking the other way.

My breath sweet as a dancing girl's, I click along, drinking in the air. A friend slows his car to offer me a ride and I thank him, decline, giggle, wave goodbye with a hysterical show of energy. He looks embarrassed and drives away.

By the time I reach town I am angry at the friend who offered the ride. I am sore because he has seen me make such a jackass of myself there on the sidewalk. What right had he to look the way he did? He might at least have suspected what I was going through, quitting cold like this after twenty-four years of fouling my lungs with the stuff. The wonderful stuff.

Well, the hell with him. With all of them. I shall stick it out another hour, and another, day by painful day until the craving subsides. The way they work it in Alcoholics Anonymous. The first cigarette is too many and a thousand cigarettes are not enough. Or something like that.

§ 42 §

I cuff another tree, this one without pleasure. It is a large oak on Courthouse Square and I reflect that it looks rottener than usual. It stirs no lyric thoughts and I am bored with deep breathing.

At this point I've been off cigarettes maybe forty-five minutes. The Man with the Golden Lungs. I wonder how many thousands of dollars in cigarettes I've sucked into and snorted out of these lungs, begging for cancer, billowing with tar-laden vapors. I blink emotionally, wondering if the canccr has already started; there is one rather sensitive place below and to the right of the wishbone. I owe it to Mary and the children to live to be at least fifty, another four years. She has enough of a load, even with Mary, Jr., and Bill away most of the time. And I think of Mary, Jr., slaving at Charity Hospital in New Orleans, where one patient, an old lady, complains during massage: "Don't rub toward my brain, girl, you're going to push all the blood into my head and give me a stroke, sure as hell." I think of Bill, so young and vulnerable, working on the paper in Oklahoma and not even able to spell very well, his heart a vacuum because the last time he came home on Christmas Eve this girl went off to church with her folks. And Kim, trying so hard to get a silver palm or whatever it is you win in the Scouts to attach to your Eagle, and his merit badges always coming unsewed from the sash and fading when they are washed. Jecca, too, needs a father a while; she could become a champion at the school of dance with her sense of balance; the first time she ever forked a bike she went all the way to Jitney Jungle before falling off on a box of seedless grapes and harelipping herself. I reflect further that Chris must be taught some guts before I depart the coil. He cannot run fast enough to be a successful coward.

The ancient U-Drive-It elevator will not come down when I press the button on the ground floor of the newspaper building. It belches and grunts in the shaft and strums its cables but does not budge.

I climb three flights of stairs, snubbing a printer and two linotype men on the way up—sane, smoking men whom ordinarily I admire. Now the sight of their cigarettes and calm thoughtful faces enrages me.

At the top of the stairs I glance at my watch and discover that an hour has passed since I got up. I figure that with the eight hours I slept and this additional hour I've already gone nine hours without smoking and that is pretty good, certainly nothing to be ashamed of, a staunch effort. After all, most of the people who manage to quit probably don't inhale. Further, if my cancer already has started, quitting now would be a matter of locking the lung after the horse, that is, the health, is gone—and if it *hasn't* already started perhaps I'm immune.

I light up—and inhale.

It is beautiful and complete and before I start the day's work I go down and apologize to the printer and the linotype men. One of them says he quit cigarettes for two whole years when he was twelve and wanted to sing in a Baptist Young People's Union choral group, but when he saw he never was going to make it he started up again.

There is a window beside my desk and when I return from downstairs I examine the fastening device. It doesn't really look altogether like a chicken gizzard, but it's better this way.

§ 44 §

The World's
Champion
Quitter

"IF I DO OR SAY ANYTHING UNREASONABLE, I'LL RIP open that pack of cigarettes and start smoking again." I leveled a shaking finger at an unopened package on the sill of the bedroom window. Morning sunlight gleamed like mother-of-pearl on the cellophane skin.

"You promise?" Mary sounded flat and exhausted.

"We can put the money I save from not smoking in a special account," I said. "More than $300 a year. It's all a matter of *relaxed* effort, this thing, you simply have to *channel* your nervousness and excess energy, make

§ 45 §

your nerves work *for* you, not against you. That's why I've failed so many times in the past. It's not enough to quit smoking, you have to quit *wanting* to smoke, see?"

She said nothing. When I talk in italics she rarely responds. Mary is a woman who is very cynical about italics.

I leaned back against the door facing, trying to look extremely good-natured. I had brushed my teeth twice since I decided to stop smoking and I had drunk two glasses of orange juice and washed out my mouth with a red liquid redolent of cinammon. My gums buzzed and I could smell my breath, oddly sharp and fragrant in the familiar air of the bedroom. I had an overwhelming desire to whirl around and smack the wall with my fist.

It was 11 A.M., a Saturday, a bright and beautiful day. I'd stubbed the last cigarette after breakfast, mashing it in the tray as if I were killing it, wanting suddenly to feel as clean and radiant as the day itself. This thing hits me every three or four months.

The phone rang in the dining room and I pivoted and galloped to answer it, making a show of channeling my energy, snatching the phone cleanly from its cradle, all of it deliberately rhythmic, in the manner of the late James Dean, who to my way of thinking was tops in channeled energy, in that no matter if he was throttling his father or driving a stolen car over a cliff, it was beautiful and balanced. The call was from my mother 250 miles away, "How are you, Son, how've you been feeling?"

"Fine," I barked. "I feel *fine*."

"You sound angry."

"Well, I'm not, I'm fine."

§ 46 §

"How're Mary and the children?"

"They're grand," I said loudly. "Why shouldn't they be?"

A long silence, then, "Son, I hope you're all right, you don't sound yourself at all, I hope you're going to church these days."

I sighed and clawed a cheek, gazing at my watch. It was only 11:10. "It's Saturday, Mother, you can't go to church on Saturday." The old familiar pressure squeezing me, the brown tobacco hunger, a blend of craving and loneliness and impending disaster.

"What?" my mother said.

"You can't find a Presbyterian church open till tomorrow," I said. "There's no damned church open, Mother. I'll go in the morning, I'll be waiting there when they open the doors."

"I hope so," she said, her voice quiet over the miles, shaming me. I wanted to tell her I was trying again to quit smoking, but she knew how many times I'd tried and I was afraid she would laugh. This final effort had to be conclusive and I knew if I surrendered now I'd never make the try again, that I'd go wheezing and hawking to my grave, a beaten man. This last stand was crucial.

"Son, do you still say your prayers?" my mother asked.

"Yes, ma'am."

"You were always such a good boy, my tenderest child, I hope you never get away from the things you believed in. You remember the time I locked you in the closet to punish you for hitting Clara Louise in the head with the roller skate; and you prayed aloud I'd let you out, and I had to open the door?"

§ 47 §

I blinked and said rapidly, "I'm all right, but I'm a little nervous."

"What's wrong, Son?"

I laughed crazily and bared my teeth at my wife, who was passing through to the kitchen. She gave me a startled glance, rolling the whites of her eyes. When she'd gone I said into the phone, "What's wrong is I want to scream and jump up and down and slap myself in the face."

"Is it anything I've said?"

"No."

"Have you been drinking?"

"No," I said. "I'm in the desert. I've been in the desert a year, twelve months, all my life. I quit drinking. I've quit everything, I'm the world's champion quitter; you know that."

"I don't understand you, Son."

"I love you, Mother." Whenever I don't know what to say to her I tell her I love her. Because it is true and although frequently, as now, it falls short of conversational brilliance, it kind of bridges the gap.

My temples felt tight and one of my jaw teeth pulsed. In the early stages of withdrawal you have some really rare sensations. The root of my tongue felt tired. I sought to rest the tongue by laying the tip of it on my lower teeth, but it gave no relief and the tiredness spread soon to the back of my neck, which I massaged with the free hand, squeezing and pinching.

"How is the writing going, Son? I mean the *other*, not at the newspaper?"

One of the things I fear most when I am trying to

quit smoking is that someone will ask me How the Writing is Going. I have the feeling that unless I smoke I'll never produce another acceptable line; that the crummy adjectives and clichés will squirt forever from my fingertips and all the good hard-hitting verbs will crouch beneath the keyboard of the aged Remington, holding their noses. "It isn't going," I said to my mother. "It isn't going at all."

I commence cuffing the wall, lightly at first, then harder.

"What's that, what's that *noise?*" she said.

"Only the wall, I'm *tapping* it." I sucked in a breath and held it. When I quit smoking I become aware of the breadth and depth of my lungs and the hundreds, perhaps thousands, of oxygen-starved air sacs. I expelled the air and inhaled a series of deep breaths. There is this dreary compulsion to ventilate every single sac.

Presently my mother hung up and I went to the bathroom and again brushed my teeth. My abused gums stung and I recalled without appreciation the gag about the fellow who said he had been to the dentist for an annual checkup and the dentist said, wonder of wonders, that he needed no new fillings and his teeth were splendid, but at the earliest opportunity he should have his gums removed. I killed another fifteen minutes tearing apart the toothpaste tube in an effort to discover the secret of the pink stripe in the paste.

Mary entered and when she saw the gutted tube pinioned against the rim of the lavatory she deposited a stack of clean towels on a shelf and backed out. Kim and Jecca came in and washed dark hands beneath the faucet of the bathtub, neither of them looking directly at me.

The phone began ringing and I flung the unsolved tube into the wastebasket, wiped my fingers and moved to answer it, still trying to channel my energy and discontent. It was the man at the gas company.

He said the bill was overdue and I said it was paid.

He suggested I find the bill, that what I'd paid a week before was for the preceding month, not the month in issue. After I located the receipt he said to look in the left-hand corner. There were the usual discouraging decimal-studded figures tangled with capital code letters. I have never really understood the printing on gas, electrical or water bills, the strange overlapping legends and dashes and dots. I am at their mercy. Now the frustration of it, combined with tobacco hunger, almost blinded me with anger.

I said finally, "I'll be *darned*, yes sir, I'll take care of it right away."

After lunch I sat on the front porch balling and un-balling my hands, tasting still the banana custard, which smells rather like fingernail polish once you're done with it.

At 1 P.M. I decided my watch was dead and I pressed it against the side of my head, surprised that it ticked. I stared at the dial a long time and the large hand, fat with phosphorus, which clings to it with the improbable bulging yellowness of wax on a bee's leg, finally registered 1:01 P.M.

I went into the bedroom and bit open the corner of the package of cigarettes and lit one. What I wanted to do was tear out both ends of the pack, ram one end in my mouth and light the other, smoking twenty cigarettes at once, deeply, and without conscience. Mary came in and kissed me. There was no talking between us about the smoking.

It was enough—for both of us—that I smoked.

§ *51* §

Classified
Adventure

THE PHONE RANG AND I AROSE FROM THE COUCH
feeling pleasantly weak.

In the dinnersmelling gloom I seized the telephone
and mashed it against my head, breathing loudly through
my nose, "Yes—yes, hallo."

A massive voice inquired, "Are you the man that's
got the '49 Plymouth for sale?"

A cool sweat tickled my ribs; this was it, the high
adventure of commerce, the teasing ruthlessness for
which I hunger. Some people get their kicks shooting

§ 52 §

large cats or ripping around a dance floor or making color photographs of their kids sitting on the incinerator; but for me there's nothing to match the excitement of answering the telephone after you've placed a classified advertisement in the newspaper. It makes no difference whether I'm hawking a tweed overcoat with bird-nest elbows, a vintage shotgun or the family's ailing second car, the vibration is there, strangely crippling, darkly lovely.

"I'm he." I try to sound amused and honest. I have learned not to commence babbling at first nibble.

"What?"

"I'm him, I'm the one."

Until I learned about classified advertisements I'd never sold anything but a few packages of cigarettes, in Japan, in the fish-smelling dark of an alley on the edge of Sendai—a crummy, shameful business which remains astride my conscience to this day. Not only was it illegal and unbecoming an American soldier, it develops in the light of later findings that I may have caused cancer among a helpless and conquered people.

This classified thing is different and decent.

It is not for the easily rattled or the faint of heart. Now, strangling with excitement, it did no good to remind myself that the sale was of little consequence; that the children would eat, and eat, and eat, regardless of the outcome.

"What you want for it?"

You know it's coming, but you're never completely ready. I loosened the phone from my ear, restoring circulation.

§ 54 §

"I'm asking two and a half."

"You're kidding."

"Two and a half firm," I said. "No offers." I hoped he would not hear my ragged breathing. The breathing is everything.

"How many miles she got on her?" He asked the question serenely. The prospective buyer never seems to have any crude problems of respiration.

"I wouldn't be afraid to start out for California in her," I evaded, accepting the conceit that the Plymouth was female.

"How's her rubber?"

"She got new sparkplugs last week," I muttered.

"She use much oil?"

I breathed more easily now, but my teeth were dry and the upper lip declined to slide properly as I shaped answer after cunning answer, "You'll be tickled with the gas, she does well on gas," I said.

"She rusted out anywhere?"

"Look," I said, eyes popped with excitement, "you slap a little wax on her and you wouldn't be ashamed to drive her to church."

I grinned, lip stuck high on the teeth, holding the phone away from my head so he would not hear me panting.

"—I tell you what," he said.

"Yes?"

"No," he said, "no, I better not. . . . But . . ."

It was excruciating, more wonderful than the summer we peddled the waffle iron to a mail carrier who kept insisting he preferred flapjacks. The phone crackled with suspense and suspicion. "You're welcome to come drive it," I said, almost sobbing with enjoyment.

Mary appeared in the room. "Is something wrong?" she asked. No matter how intent she is on what she's doing she finds time to pose this, her favorite question.

"Well," the man said, "I'm not making any promises, but I *may* get in touch with you."

"Fine."

"Sure you wouldn't come down to, say, two hundred?"

"Is something *wrong*?" Mary stared at my dry, bare teeth.

"No," I said to her.

"Is that a final answer?" the man wanted to know.

"Something *is* wrong," Mary said.

"NO," I roared at her.

"Ah, the hell with it," the man said and hung up.

That was two weeks ago and I haven't had a decent nibble on the old Plymouth since. A woman phoned last night. She wanted to talk to someone about a '49 Plymouth her uncle owned when she was a kid; and how they used to drive it to Lake Shady to swim and it took to the woods like a jeep, jumping stumps and squirming out of mudholes. It was what she called a fun car, loose-jointed and raffish, nine different colors of dark blue like dried ink or the sun shining on a rooster's tail, and everything bumping and thumping and rattling so that you couldn't pick out any single noise to worry yourself sick about.

No, she didn't want to buy a '49 Plymouth, the ad just reminded her of that other one and the grand times at Lake Shady. Her uncle couldn't even swim, she added.

She did say, however, that she had a brother in service who was crazy about old Plymouths and he was getting his discharge in the summer.

I do not believe I can keep the Plymouth alive until summer.

Snake
Music

MARY CAME ONTO THE FRONT PORCH AND THUMPED beside me on the couch. "Oh, there you are, all sunk down in your sweater."

I ignored her because I dislike for her to say there I am, all sunk down in my sweater, or shirt, or whatever. When you are forty-six and ripe in all the wrong places the law of gravity is something to be reckoned with, not joked about.

She begins whistling. She has a pleasant speaking voice, but her whistle sounds like snake music. After a time she tires of it. "I'm sorry about not being forty," she says.

"Oh, that's all right." I yawn my indifference. It is pleasantly cool on the porch and I've been sitting there watching the cars go by and thinking of the way she tricked me about her birthday. It does not matter if it has been done deliberately or not. There is treachery in it, an absolute lack of consideration.

"I really thought I was *going* to be," she says.

"Forget it." I fondle the chest of the sweater, which is an off-brown, swamp-water shade, certainly a proper color for sinking into. It is a gift from Mary's mother, who is fond of dressing me in brown although it makes me look like a Kodiak bear.

Throughout the past year Mary has led me to believe that she is going to be forty. She must have sensed what it meant to me. Then on her birthday, two days ago, she said she'd discovered she was only thirty-nine. It was absurd from any angle. People don't go around *discovering* how old they are any more than they *discover* their middle names or great toes.

When I laughed at her "discovery" she documented it with her birth certificate, parched and amber, which she said she'd found at the bottom of a cigar box full of dried crickets and orange peel in Kim's bureau. The boy testified the certificate was not a forgery, that he'd had it as long as he could recall, bringing it with him when we moved from New Orleans and again from Denver.

In the light of this development it was apparent Mary wasn't quite eighteen when we'd married, a thing I must have known a long time ago when we were kissing as long as thirty minutes at a whack unless one of us suffered a cold and could not breathe through the nose, but a fact which was none the less shocking, dredged up like this from a forgotten box of juiceless bugs.

I did not so much resent the fact, that she wasn't forty as I did the way she had gone about not *becoming* forty.

The ultimate deception had been fermenting for years, possibly decades, since I could recall that last year we celebrated her thirty-ninth birthday and the year before, the thirty-eighth.

Since November of 1956 I'd been in the forties all alone and had looked forward to her joining me; not because I am vicious, mind you, although it is true that the minute I myself hit forty (without delay or subterfuge) I commenced getting even fatter and purpler and grayer, and on occasion men in their late thirties called me sir.

Actually, although I anticipated it, it struck me that her pending fortieth birthday was not without an element of tender melancholy. I looked up the word "matron" in the dictionary and it said any wife or widow was a matron, especially one who had borne children. This was rather unsatisfactory for purposes of nostalgic research, but there was another definition which seemed to hit the nail on the head and to describe what Mary would be from this point forward: *a staid and motherly woman.*

She was less than amused at the definition; and I'm not criticizing her, but she became increasingly less amused as her birthday loomed and I continued quoting the passage from *Webster's New International Diction-ary*, second edition, unabridged.

Her resistance to aging only made me feel the more affectionate.

In truth I was so moved by it I went downtown and bought more presents than she had got for Christmas, a gleaming mess of household appliances and an expensive pin shaped like a bumblebee. I spent, and charged, and laid away, and budget-planned threefold as much as I would have if I'd known she was only bearing down on thirty-nine—a nondescript and unremarkable age, little more than a neutral ground between youth and decay.

You can understand why later I calculated she'd conned me.

Now, on the couch on the porch, she said: "I'll be forty next year. Surely you can wait that long."

"I don't know," I said. "Sometimes my chest hurts." I stared at the cars whizzing by. None of the people in the cars seemed to be over forty and not many of them beyond thirty.

"You'll bury us all." She leaned sideways against me. "Sure."

"You think too much about getting *old* and *ailing*," she said. "You get a little gas in your chest and you bolt up in bed in the middle of the night and scare me half to death. I'm ready to phone for oxygen."

That washed it.

I arose and lumbered into the house and spent the next five minutes raking my scalp with a stiff brush, trying to raise the prow of my crewcut, which insists on lying flat as Caesar's. I considered and rejected the idea of trying to fasten the fig-shaped punching bag to the ceiling of the back porch.

I could hear her whistling on the porch the snake music.

Lotus
Trouble

MY EYES BURN BRIGHT AS PIGEON-BLOOD RUBIES FROM standing on my head and capillaries in the farthest reaches of a cholesterol-clogged circulatory system are once again open to traffic.

For I have discovered Yoga, a mystic way of life which for more than twenty centuries has beckoned mankind.

Within scant months I've attained a state of rigid mental clarity which enables me to recall my home telephone number, the month of the year, my favorite brand

of cheese straws. Further, I am supple as a snake except for certain problems of sitting which will be explained later.

Some time ago I became actively interested in Yoga when I saw a movie magazine photograph of Marlon Brando smoldering on one leg, holding his breath and staring straight ahead with great burning eyes. I did not know at the time that all Yogis have burning eyes because all of them are required to get onto their heads at least twice a day, and preferably three times. If they cannot endure this they must turn in their breechclouts and nail-studded sleeping boards and dried fruit.

Brando balanced there, brooding in a black leotard, and the stance, for all its storklike angularity, had an air of rightness about it.

I began combing the area for a Yoga book and can say candidly that Yoga isn't likely to catch on down here in the deep South where even the Ivy League Look had a cruel fight for acceptance and not even the Republican party has been able to get any kind of hold on the imagination of the people. In any event, last winter the books were located, three of them, in a college library; and the same night I began devouring them, experimenting with that of the lotus.

You may as well understand from the start that the hardest thing a Yogi does is sit down.

But don't be overly optimistic. They call the official position the "lotus seat" and the discouraging truth is that one must place his feet in his lap. Even when I was a tad and used to play jacks with my girl cousins I could not with any comfort sit on the floor and at the same time get my feet out of the way of the rubber ball. As for the lotus seat, I am able to hoist the left foot into place, but cocking it there locks some mysterious vertebra at the base of my spine and the other foot won't budge for any stimulus short of surgery.

At this writing I remain approximately a half-lotus short of perfection. Some days I lose ground and cannot hoist even the left foot. This must be mental, or, again, it may be poisons from the broiled meats which I can't seem to renounce despite the fact that a Yogi of the first class would rather take a severe beating than square off with a sirloin strip.

On one occasion I became bitterly impatient, seized the right foot and jerked it toward my lap, a grievous error which cured me permanently of trying to hurry this thing. I felt as if I'd been bitten in the groin by a bulldog.

In brighter vein I can report that holding my breath (here again, like headstanding, *all* Yogis do it, nor do they for a moment question it) came easy, because my wife turned teetotaler a while back after observing what she described as my "progressive merriment" at a New Year's Eve party. Since she quit drinking she can smell a shot of vodka over a long-distance telephone connection, whether person-to-person or station-to-station. Thus, long before Yoga I'd learned to greet her of an evening upon arriving home from the job, kiss her, remove my jacket, find a chair and unfold the newspaper before exhaling the rich, telltale contents of my lungs.

The Yogi headstand is somewhat hairier to master than the not breathing and if you are unwary it may toss you tail over teakettle into the gate-leg table. This causes various complications and, generally speaking, is not well received by the more responsible members of the family. In point of fact, such awkwardness defeats the very purpose of Yoga, which is to free you from pain and worry. In February I hurt my toe and lost two weeks of practice while it healed and it may be stated without fear of contradiction that although hospital insurance is not a necessity for the Yogi, it helps.

It elates me to tell you in closing that the rewards of the thing outweigh cost in bodily comfort and today I can stand on one leg like Marlon Brando. With me there is more belly and less controlled-fire than with Brando, but, as I tell my wife, he wears those flattering black tights.

Hypnotism
in the Home

AFTER ONLY A WEEK OF STUDYING HYPNOTISM I FIND that I am able to make the subject's eyes water. In a single night I made Mary's eyes water and also Jecca's. Jecca's nose watered, too, but this is characteristic of her at certain times of the year and I take no credit for it.

It is only honest to point out that the production of body fluids is hardly the ultimate goal of hypnotism, but it serves as a starter and the books I'm reading promise me that within the month I shall be able to plummet the subject into that state known as Deep Trance.

§ 68 §

If you are really interested in hypnotism in the home, an area relatively unexplored to date, here's how you go about it, and keep in mind the heartening fact that it requires no great store of animal magnetism.

First you must have something to dangle three or four inches and slightly above the eyes of the subject. The eyes must be rolled upward to see the object and this alone will cause slight watering if you stick with it long enough. One book advises dangling a crystal ball filled with blue-dyed sand, but don't bother looking for such a ball, because as far as I can determine they are no longer in production.

The best of all devices, I understand, even superior to the container of blue sand, is a clear glass ball pierced by a steel pin, the end of which is surmounted by a tiny glittering nickel-plated sphere. I should think that locating one of these would be a greater triumph than becoming the champion of hypnotists.

I compromise by wadding up some tinfoil one of the kids had thrown in the bathtub after eating a Hershey bar. I tied a length of dental floss around it and suspended it in the prescribed position and informed Mary that sleep was creeping all over her. She yawned and smiled.

"Your eyes are very heavy," I said. "They want to roll back in your head. Your arms and legs are tired."

"True," she said.

"You are at *peace* with the world."

This sent her into gales of laughter, after which she subsided into a mood of extreme quiet, a single tear glistening high on her right cheek. Later she said the tear was from laughing. It is characteristic of a subject

that he or she will minimize the power of the hypnotist. This is plainly stated by the experts who wrote the books.

Jecca began nodding after only a minute or two of staring at the foil from the Hershey and both her eyes began watering, small streams polishing pathways down her pale cheeks. She said later that as she gazed at the ball of tinfoil she imagined that it was the entire world, oceans rocking and sloshing, all that black water with sharks and God knew whatall rocking inside it, and her eyelids became terribly heavy. She said she saw herself dancing on the ocean and she wore pink satin ballet slippers of the best quality. At one point in my experiment with her, impatient to achieve deep trance, I reached out and pinched shut her lids. This, of course, is cheating and anyway she immediately opened her nearsighted powder-blue eyes and her concentration was shattered.

Already I have learned the hard way that vast patience, as well as willpower, is required of the hypnotist and that he must at all costs preserve an air of self-confidence, a certain bearing which, combined with the mystery of the thing and proper lighting, gives him what the Masters describe as *prestige*. Thousands of years ago Egyptian masters who hadn't even been to college were able to control both pain and bleeding by means of hypnotism and prestige. When those lads said an artery was going to stop squirting, well, it stopped as if somebody had twisted a nozzle. It's all in the record, don't take my word for it.

If there is a single naked light bulb in the room and this shines directly into the eyes of the subject, so much the better. I was surprised to learn that the more uncomfortable the subject's eyes, the more favorable for the hypnotist; and that almost any trick short of sandpapering the eyeballs is acceptable to the trade.

Chris was a bitter disappointment to me in my experiments. An imaginative child, in fact the only six-year-old I know who worries about God not getting any sleep ("He's workin' all the time, he's got to make it rain and make it thunder and lightnin' "), I believed Chris would lend himself perfectly as a subject, since sensitivity is vital. I advised him that his right arm was becoming rigid. After ordering him to thrust the arm straight out from his body I hissed: "Every muscle in your arm is *rigid,* they are becoming more and more *rigid,* your hand, your very fingers are rigid and you cannot bend the arm —YOU CANNOT BEND IT!"

He dropped the arm. "What's *rigid?*" he asked.

You may expect setbacks in the beginning, but the book declares that as skill and prestige grow you will be able to plunge pins into subjects and they will know very little, if anything, about it. You are advised not to be absent-minded in this regard, and to always remove the pins and other pointed objects before releasing the subject from trance because most unhypnotized people are startled when they note that such things are being pulled out of them.

This is the part I'm waiting for; not because I am a congenitally spiteful man, but because I am weary of the ridicule and slapstick and doubting, the uncalled-for and concerted effort to discourage me so that these smoldering energies may be diverted to carrying out the garbage and cutting the grass.

§ 72 §

When I began this study I had no desire to stick a pin into a single member of my family; and even now, after the days of persecution and withering laughter, I realize a need for continued patience and thoughtfulness.

I shall *sterilize* the pins.

Alka-Seltzer
in the Blackberry

Juice

I CAN'T IMAGINE WHY IT IS THAT AS YOU GROW OLDER people become less interested in you.

Because it isn't until you're solidly into your forties that you can discuss with reflection and mature intelligence the shatteringly important matters of sleep and digestion. You've accumulated a lush fund of stories about the human belly, how it functions, what soothes or riles it. You know stark little stories about men who died within seconds after ingesting boiled rutabaga. You are competent to discourse on the significance of removing the slimy underskin of a broiled flounder and can talk for hour after golden hour on the belch, its causes, virtues and drawbacks.

And along the way you have compiled remarkable statistics on calories and cholesterol, plus an acute and untiring interest in body weight. You know from day to day your exact poundage, to the fraction, stripped or dressed, fed or empty.

All in all you become a treasure trove of fascinating facts and intimate revelations about your personal plumbing and the secret movements therein. And this is only the half of it; you know how many hours of sleep you got last night and the night before and possibly last New Year's Eve, when Fred drank the dirty water from the tray while the icebox was being defrosted. In these knowing years you are not content to achieve eight hours of unconsciousness, you are compelled to share with friends and family your *methods* of sleeping. You do not flop into bed and begin snoring in the manner of some callow youth, you pursue sleep slyly, with pill and stretching exercise ("Well, first I stretch all the toes on my right foot, I mean I really stretch *hell* out of 'em. . . .")

You'd think people would find this sort of thing absorbing, but you begin to note a deadness around their eyes when you talk to them. This deadness is not confined to the eyes alone, but appears to paralyze the skin for inches around the sockets.

Your wife no longer tells the kids they will grow up to be like you, since two have already grown and are not in the least like you, and of the remainder, one is a girl and the others seem too busy to care. When you rattle out of the house with the golf clubs no one even looks up from the TV.

The other night during a brief drive in the country Mary was admiring the sky, raggedy clouds sailing in moonlight. When I observed that the moon looked like an Alka-Seltzer floating in a bowl of dietetic blackberry juice she broke into almost hysterical laughter.

I mean, it wasn't healthy wholesome laughter at all.

She continued snorting without explanation all the way home and expressed no wish to prolong the drive, giving the impression of relief when it was done with. She used to love our aftersupper tours while the children were doing homework and would plead with me to stretch them longer and longer.

I don't know.

I suspect that neither she, nor my listless, rapidly cooling friends, are getting enough sleep.

Devilish
Destiny
of a Golf Ball

AFTER HAGGARD MONTHS OF TRYING TO MASTER THE game of golf it is my opinion that the real thrill of it (as it is now played) is finding your ball.

A man playing a game involving a ball should be able to take the presence of the ball for granted and go on from there. Even in football, where deception is at a premium, relatively little strength is spent looking for the ball; it may vanish briefly but everyone knows that in any event it will be available for the next play.

Not so with golf, not a bit of it.

§ 77 §

The enthusiasts sing of the slamming *whock* of Snead's woods and the clean *whick* of iron against high-test rubber and gutta-percha. A friend who on his better days gnaws nervously at the fringes of par tells me in all seriousness that the sweet music of a good drive is superior to the sight of the ball, even to the ball in actual flight, when it is not headed for woods or any other hiding place, "*It sounds like a sack of buckshot whamming a concrete wall—no noise like it.*"

Well, for me there's no more refreshing experience, or rewarding spectacle, after a hike through bramble and scrub oak, than just finding my ball. I don't care if it sounded like a sack of jellybeans and chop suey when I hit it.

I'm capable of losing it in the middle of the fairway. At times, if the fairway is broad and sun-dazzled, it's tougher than in the shade of the woods, where the paleness of the ball (occasionally) leaps out in pure contrast. Also, there are wadded empty cigarette packets on the fairways and I have been known to walk an eighth of a mile to refresh my knowledge regarding the fact that Winston's possess finer filter for finer flavor. A balled-up Chesterfield pack gives an even more faithful impersonation of the missing ball. All in all I guess I prefer the off-fairway game because I've had more practice in the forest and have beaten deep and useful trails there.

Once I lost a ball on the edge of a green in what Jimmy Demaret calls frog-hair on TV. It was an old ball, scarred deeply on one cheek and stained chartreuse from violent association with juicy grasses. I'd found it earlier in a combination ditch-pond where its true owner lost it or threw it away.

This latter explanation is due since I myself never keep a ball long enough to stain it.

If I play a ball for seven holes or more I feel a bewildered affection for it and its ultimate loss is the more wrenching. You know how you feel about a raincoat or umbrella which contrives to remain un-lost through an entire winter. The broad honest face of the club professional may be said to glow when I enter the clubhouse. Off the golfing premises he doesn't like me particularly and it's certain he admires neither my game nor equipment, this last carried in a limp canvas quiver, innocent of pull cart or stylish mittens, clubheads clustered nakedly in sparse bouquet, rusty as hybrid carnations.

What the pro likes about me is I'm chronically and dependably fresh out of golf balls.

He's kind enough to consider appearances in that he rarely laughs outright while selling me a new carton. Maybe he sold me a new box of the things only a half-hour ago, but aside from an exaggeratedly pleasant expression you'd never guess it to look at him.

On Father's Day and other special and ludicrous occasions I treat myself to several of the very best balls. These appear more heavily enameled than the others and the tinted dots and lettering are in rarer color and the cellophane on the face of the carton somewhat cracklier. But until the PGA gets around to approving concession of long shots off the tee (I understand that at present they won't even endorse conceding two-foot putts) I recommend to the beginner the 70¢ ball. It does not lose itself so nimbly as the attractive $1.25 ball. Of course this is a matter of degree, not a *solution*.

My golfing companions, who include a carpenter, a

preacher and a man who operates a machine that clamps the little metal prongs on Manila envelopes, generally locate their own balls without fuss. They have suggested that I line up the flight of the ball with a special tree or bush on the rim of the fairway. This is not easy with a screaming slice which in the course of flight may at one time or another be in line with every growing thing in the sector and also with inanimate objects like the spire of the First Methodist, a low-hanging cloud shaped like a breast and a torn yellow kite hung on a power line. As for using any kind of tree as a point of orientation, the ball ricochets *off* them.

Further, a tree at two hundred yards does not look like the same tree when you reach it and stand at its base.

An ugly miracle transpires. Other trees of similar shape, diameter and foliage spring up all round it. As these additional trees commence to lunge out of the earth you get the old feeling, sweaty and hopeless and lost, almost panicky. You wheel and continue walking, backward now; maybe you've overwalked the ball and will find it in azimuth.

You dread going so soon again to the clubhouse where the new balls lie tamely in the glass case. You wonder how many of the fellows are still there—that is, how many of the ones who were there when you bought the last carton of balls.

The lost ball, your last one, snuggles secretly in its bower, secure, successful. It has fulfilled its date with destiny, which, from the moment the rubber was milked from the mother tree on the Malay Peninsula, was to hijack you for the better part of a dollar or more, to twang your nerves and sicken your heart.

§ *81* §

I've found that before you learn the unnatural trick of keeping your head down during a tee shot things go slightly better, since you are able to observe the flight of the ball from its beginning.

Nowadays I glimpse only the final flirt of the slice as it enters the jungle and this affords the ball all the advantage. As if the damned thing needed any.

By way of conclusion and review, if you're a fairly average man on a golf course and you're out for some fun, not a lesson in woodcraft or automation, never turn your back on the ball. No matter what anybody says, allow your head to rotate smoothly with the clubhead when stroking. Aside from visual benefits, this lubricates and eases the all-important follow-through, making it more natural and protecting the vertebrae against backlash.

Select yourself a partner mature and relaxed enough to concede you a towering drive down the middle when the fairways are dangerously tight. I say any joker, the PGA notwithstanding, has mettle enough to concede you a dinky six-inch putt.

Perhaps you won't crack par.

But time and again you'll know golf's most basic thrill: you'll know where your *ball* is.

Strange
How
Tennis
Has Changed

RECENTLY, AND TEMPORARILY, I DESPAIRED OF GOLF and on a glistening hot afternoon decided to resume a habit known as tennis.

In tennis the addict moves about a hard rectangle and seeks to ambush a fuzzy ball with a modified snow-shoe. There is a net in the middle of the court and often you can find the ball at the base of this net—a convenience denied golfers.

The primary conception of tennis is to get the ball over the net and at the same time to keep it within bounds

§ 83 §

of the court; failing this, within the borders of the neighborhood.

For the man of years there are three main strokes: forehand, backhand and sun.

Before this account attains full focus I wish to call attention to the fact I had not played the game for six years. I had not played it well in twenty and maybe I never did. Like the man said, I'm not the man I used to be and never *was*. I have been smoking two packages of cigarettes daily and trying to break in a rack of pipes which my wife believes are becoming to, if not mandatory for, a writer.

Also, I am so extravagantly built, despite sporadic dieting, that when I brake to a dead halt in rubber-soled shoes my middle slings forward long after the feet are stilled. During ensuing moments, centrifugal force and retraction tear at the flesh beneath my T-shirt and I may be said to shimmy.

With what amounted to less than cunning I chose as my opponent for this afternoon a man who neither smokes, drinks nor shimmies.

He too is plump, but his burden is more wholesome and disciplined. It moves with him in whatever direction he desires and does not seem in any way to conflict with his footwork or breathing.

During the preliminary warmup I discovered that to indulge in the habit of tennis one must run many times, never very far in any single direction, but continuously in countless directions. This had slipped my mind. I'd recalled simply the striking of the ball from various, rather photogenic, angles; transportation didn't enter into it at all. You were here. You were there. You hit the ball. Now and then you called out, "Fine shot, beautiful, really!"

The truth is (and heed this if you plan renewal of the game you enjoyed as a colt), you must strain every valve and vessel to the limit of its guaranty to earn the privilege of hacking at the ball. Indeed, you must swim rivers of sweat, burn scarlet scabs on your nose in the sun and run, run, run. And I don't mean the whimsical or gracious kind of running one does from patio to telephone.

Gone is the insolent floating grace of yesteryear, the light clean loping and hard-curving stroke. After slogging eight desperate paces to meet the ball you're too whacked to care if the shot is crisp and well placed.

And the serve.

Remember the glow you used to get when your service came around, the fresh steel of forearm, shoulder and calf? You didn't even have to think about it. You pondered your suntan, your date for the evening and the achingly beautiful prospect of Swiss steak and butter beans for supper.

Sometimes you barely realized you'd served until the ball hissed over the taped rim of the net.

That's all different now, I find.

When I cranked up, there was a bleak crunch in the working shoulder, the sort of thing one hears when cutting a deck of lettuce with the edge of a fork.

Simply getting up high on the ball of the left foot proved a test of balance and calf sinew, the racket handle slick in my fist, eyes stinging with the fluids of exhaustion.

Twice I threw the ball too high and lost it in the sun

on my service. Someone snickered on the next court. I believe it was a teen-age girl for whom I'd been trying to hold in my stomach. There is no question she had a right to laugh. On another occasion I tossed up two balls at once and stepped on the third and did a quarter-split.

At game's end my companion leaped the net the way they do in the newsreels and without looking me in the eye said he was tired. "Let's take a break," he said. "It's hot out here." He breathed evenly and moved all of a piece and there was barely a button of sweat on him.

I tried to smile. "All right."

We walked to a wooden practice wall at the end of the line of courts and sat down, leaning against the wood, he still trying manfully to look exhausted, neither of us saying much; and it hit me then with a sorrowful slap what time had done to a machine which only a handful of years ago had brimmed with energy and careless strength. Suddenly one day you leaned against a wooden wall and knew you were a slob.

Nevertheless, I may—I'm not pledging myself, but I just may—try it again. I have thought it out at length and believe that if comfort and self-satisfaction are the things that destroy a man, tennis might well be the key to eternal health.

A Man's
Lawn
Is
His Undoing

I SAT DOWN IN THE DIRT FEELING VERY OLD AND
chilled and tired as the sweat dried tightly along the skin
of my spine. I looked at my right arm and it did seem
swollen. Perhaps something important and difficult to
spell was torn loose in there. Perhaps I'd write Mary,
Jr., at nursing school and ask her about it, but I flinched
from this because once she told me that she was a dis-
ciple of the straight and uncluttered diagnosis and that
she admired most the doctor who looked the patient in ·
the eye and said, "Three months, I give you three at the
outside."

§ 88 §

"When you raise the hatchet up and swing it down it makes your arm swell out kind of funny," Kim said, squatting beside me. "But maybe it's just muscle."

Four solid hours I'd been there in the yard, spreading topsoil, planting grass, hammering. Kim had been picking up the wee broken roots that came in the load of topsoil and he could not understand why I was bushed.

"You reckon it's muscle?" he said.

I sneezed. "No, son, it's my gardening glands."

"Now you're kidding," he said. I was grateful that he did not choose the moment to laugh his official Scout guffaw.

I arose and picked up the hatchet and hammered in two more stakes with the butt of it, continuing to build a pathetic little fence around the tender seed. We have the only solid terra-cotta yard in town with the exception of the fire station. Driving a stake into this slab is a job for a younger man, a man of more reliable metabolism. Blue-steel circles and orange picnic plates sailed before my eyes as I hammered.

"You're mighty purple in the jaws," said Kim. He picked up a root and stared at it. Then, with no effort at transition he said: "In school we're studying about the first men, you know, the Java man, the Heidelberg and Neanderthal fellas. I always thought Adam was kind of handsome and that Eve was a good-looking babe, but if the scientists are right, well, Adam must've looked kind of like a baboon. And Eve, too. I don't know why Adam would risk so much trouble and give up all that free fruit and stuff in the Garden of Eden to get in Eve's pants, or fur, or whatever."

"I don't know," I said, which was the truth. I felt

awful and didn't care if Adam had fangs a foot long and Eve had a breath that would kill a tree and hair under her arms that reached all the way to the ground.

"Well, look," said Kim, unwilling to let loose of it, mainly because it kept him from having to pick up roots, but I imagine partly because it was a sexual subject after a fashion, and at his age he is not too choosy in that area. He will, if you give him your attention, spend an hour discussing the Rebel Chick-Sexing Service, which is operated by a kindly Japanese who separates males from females shortly after they emerge from the egg, a task both delicate and important, but not exactly lurid and certainly not especially stimulating to most laymen.

"You go look," I said, "for those *roots.*"

"The thing that worries me," said Kim over his shoulder, "is if the Lord made Adam in His own image and Adam looked like a—"

"Shut up," I said. "You make me nervous."

With four stakes in the ground and eight to go I was at the end of my endurance. My arm felt pulpy. It quivered against my wet ribs.

I sat again on the ground and at this point Mary and Chris and Jecca came onto the front porch, settling themselves in sling chairs, the three of them eying me thoughtfully.

A car door slammed in the street and one of Jecca's friends came tripping along the walk, cheeks bright with the artistic exertions of ballet. She carried the seedy little bag in which all of Jecca's pals apparently tote their ballet slippers and dancing tights. "The yard looks beautiful," she lied on her way to the porch.

§ *90* §

The yard was a sea of clay dumplings where I'd tried to rake and water, to manufacture dirt.

"The yard," I said, "looks like hell."

Jecca's friend smiled and nodded and went onto the porch, busy with the birdlike thoughts of a ballerina. I heard her telling Jecca that she had been named to dance the part of the scarecrow in a recital. Jecca and Mary squealed as if being a scarecrow was a big break. It was clear to me that none of them really cared about me or the yard. A cool wind blew across my backbone. What if I found it impossible now to arise from the dirt? Would they leave me here, lame and beaten, an unloved figure glued forever to the sod? Kim would wolf my share of the liver and onions, wipe his glistening lips on the necktie I'd loaned him. My eyes prickled with self-pity.

It was getting dark when finally I pried myself loose from the earth.

Kim was gone and no one was on the porch. Jecca's ballerina friend had departed with her bag and slippers and lambswool. Somehow I drove the remaining stakes, strung the wire and fastened to it the rag flags. As I did this I faced a few simple truths: the fact that the yard probably would not nourish weeds, much less Bermuda; the old house (undoubtedly a gourmet's delight for termites) would be eaten to the eaves by the time the last payment was made; and Jecca would continue to invite bag-swinging ballerina propagandists until she had her way about the ballet lessons. It was more important to Jecca to pack her toes in wool and go stumbling about a stage than it was to have grass or food or even oxygen.

I hobbled into the house.

Mary had my bath water running hot and clear and

the table was set in the dining room instead of the kitchen and there was a place for me. I noted the chipped plate was at Kim's place and that my own plate was without blemish.

"Darling," said Mary, "you take all the time you want for your bath—we'll eat when you're ready." She smelled faintly of liver and onions. She added that anyone who worked as hard as I'd worked deserved special treatment.

At supper, still bemused by her calculated and rather corny solicitude, my right arm dead as a doornail, I waved my fork and babbled. I told them how easy it was to plant grass and drive stakes. I told them how grand I felt from the exercise and they nodded and beamed and laughed happily, as if they were proud to have such a zippy old mule for a father and husband. "You ought to see the guy's muscle," Kim said, only a glint of cynicism in his long blue eyes. "Really," he said.

I guess it went to my head.

Anyway, I've signed up for all kinds of things next weekend in the back yard—rip up a patch of cane, plant a yew hedge and mimosa, cut the grass, and drop dead.

Anybody
Can Be
a Writer

EVERY NOW AND THEN I QUIT MY NEWSPAPER JOB TO work as a real Writer and during the process of composing four books and numerous short stories and articles for the magazine trade I've learned, rather against my will, that three out of five citizens are convinced they could bat out a crusher of a novel if only they had the time, energy and enough paper.

And the funny thing is—if indeed there is a funny thing to be derived from this—they could.

A novel is, after all, nothing more than a fairly long story; and if you chunk too many characters into it and

§ 94 §

they commence to confuse you, they may be written into a boat ride and drowned. Some authors prefer hurricanes, blizzards or epidemics.

In any event, if you produced three pages a day for six months you'd have yourself 540 pages, and that is plenty of book in any company.

Cost of the paper, if you don't insist on the very best, shouldn't run over five dollars. Throw in a couple of typewriter ribbons, a blip of Murine and a small box of aspirin and, providing you own a machine, your novel will cost you about $8.80. As a matter of fact, it's almost cheaper to write one than to buy one in hard cover.

The absolutely marvelous thing, even more impressive than the economy of it, is that once the book is begun you become a Writer. And when you've become a Writer in the eyes of your friends and neighbors you may wear bushy suits woven of mud and twigs and stare out the window for as long as you please. Windows are indispensable to the Writer who sincerely enjoys the game. Very few persons are brazen or headlong enough to barge in and interrupt a writer who is looking out of a window.

Under no circumstances say anything about what you see beyond the glass. Concede your audience the privilege of *guessing* at what you see and think. This is the way they prefer it, and they will credit you with some dandies because they are convinced your creative musings are constantly on the wing. It is not like when a certified public accountant or a plain millionaire looks out the window to see if they should wear their galoshes. And it doesn't matter that what you're really thinking is that you would like to remove a shoe and scrape your toes on the shag rug.

An English pipe, perhaps a Dunhill, is excellent for overall tone on such occasions; and at least one slightly used Irish setter is recommended if you can bear the traffic of feeding and smelling and scratching it. For some unexplained reason you can place, let us say, a panda in a room with an Irish setter and the panda looks as if he could write blazingly good copy.

In fairness to your public, and I do not refer to members of your family, who know you much too intimately for this kind of fakery to stay on the rails, train your mind in the matter of picturesque word patterns.

This isn't as hard as you might think.

Simply shake up a few of the old ones and refer coolly to such items as eye-blue skies, hair-colored wheat, or lip-colored cherries. That will get them every time despite the obvious fact it is nothing but a cliché turned wrong-side out. When you're sprinkling the lawn or washing the car, try to envision little silver hyphens instead of plain droplets of water. Remember, now that you're a Writer there are scores of people depending on you to think pretty.

Getting published may present a mild hitch, but don't let this phase of it depress you. If you play it properly the whole thing is between you and the publisher and no one need know that the publisher considers your efforts embarrassingly static, without apparent point, devoid of message, and lacking in warmth.

When friends press you for a progress report, pinch your lip and find a window to gaze out of. One of the more effective and titillating evasions is, "No, I haven't heard anything *lately*—it's still on the fire."

They like to think of your work writhing brilliantly

in the publisher's crucible and the image, scintillant and tough and vague, appears to satisfy them for years on end.

As for your actual writing, which plays only the puniest part in the process of enjoying the business of being a Writer, be sure that the first three or four words are eye-catching ones. What I mean is, whomp up a fascinating title. Everybody knows Tennessee Williams has used the better ones; but if you sweat it a bit you can come up with something like *"Wild Pigs and Blue Hydrangeas,"* or *"Molita."*

In fact, you can have those.

As the months pass, your buddies, as well as the clear-eyed and unintimidated members of your family, will shorten the title for purposes of conversation and correspondence. They'll say, "Well, how're we comin' along with *Pigs*?" Or, "What do we hear from *Moe*?" You get used to this and they mean no harm.

Fasten your mind to the bald, beautiful knowledge that they're interested in you and in the high-blown glamour of your Writing program—also that they, too, can become novelists providing they have the urge, the window, and $8.80.

As the John
Leans
So Leans
the Family

THREE MONTHS AGO MARY SAID A PORTION OF THE bathroom floor had become unsteady if not dangcrous. This was complicated by the fact that the toilet was bolted to this patch of floor and when one reached for anything or flipped the pages of a magazine the entire complex of planks, linoleum and porcelain, yawed and shivered.

I'd noticed the situation some time earlier but preferred the rodeo-rider act to the idea of wiping out our life savings of $83. No matter, I contacted a friend who is a fireman and part-time plumber. He slid under the house and scuffled around a long time and when he came out he said the termites were so thick he thought they were going to chew the handle off his hammer; that all the flooring under the toilet should be replaced before somebody got hurt.

It was decided that as long as we must have this done we might as well have the entire bathroom floor re-covered, in sassy black-and-white asphalt tile.

My friend the fireman said he could swing the whole job for $125. He is, or rather was, a cheerful man and his confidence was contagious. He is the kind of man who smiles in such a way that when you look at him you can't imagine any further toilet trouble. One day he came in his little truck, not the fire truck but a battered Mediterranean blue one with a kind of bed in the back. When he began ripping out the old floor it was a thrilling thing. Finally, after he had laid about him right and left with his crowbar, he pulled the toilet up by its mysterious roots and then there he stood on the ground, just head and shoulders protruding above the floor where the toilet was.

Within eight hours he and his assistant had a new patch of flooring down, covered with plywood and the black-and-white tile; and he had restored the toilet, which by now was sorely-needed.

The toilet was as shaky as ever, but after being without it all day, and considering its new environment, you didn't mind as much as before. It still jumped and now it clattered its lid when you came near it, but floating on the patch on black and white squares it shone fashion-ably. Only a third of the room was covered with the black and white tile because I really did have to use the bathroom pretty badly and, too, it appeared wiser to wait until we had the cash to cover the rest. While we saved for this the new squares began curling at the edges like dead fingernail clippings.

Each day a new section came unstuck.

We called the fireman back four or five times on the days he was not fighting fires and he came uncomplainingly and smilingly and spread new glue and said now it would be all right. He said he'd fixed his own bathroom and it looked like something you'd see in a catalog. This was comforting but of no real value to us. We continued calling him back with his bucket of glue until he barely smiled at all and never mentioned his own bathroom, of which he was understandably proud.

Finally the section of tile at the toilet end of the room appeared either stuck or too tired to raise itself and by this time we'd saved enough money to tile the rest of the place. Our toilet habits by now were geared to the fireman's work schedule, which is to say that every other day, when he was fighting flames, we went to the bathroom just as other people do.

To tighten a tragic account, let us say simply that he tiled the rest of the bathroom and it didn't come off. Or we should say, rather, it did. Individually and in twos and threes the squares popped free of the glue, jutting starkly. "I swear," the fireman would say, "I don't understand it." This unnerved us because we felt that if he himself didn't grasp the problem, we had little chance of recovery.

The phone calls were resumed. It got to a point where he sounded almost terrified. A patch beneath the space-heater arose from the ooze, lifting with it the tiny heater.

Another area came to life along the edge of the tub. "I just swear," the fireman said without mirth or optimism, "I just *swear*."

He was so depressed and challenged he strode into the yard and returned with a 50-pound slab of broken concrete, plunking it atop freshly-stuck squares: "Pressure," he told us. "We need pressure."

In the following weeks the original section around the john joined the uprising and when I came home from the office one night I was astonished at the size and texture of the latest concrete slab which nosed the base of the toilet. Now, to sit on the thing (the toilet) it was necessary to assume the pose of Rodin's great work, The Thinker. I am not against thinking on the toilet and suspect many truly significant thoughts occur there, but this was not smooth concrete on the floor. There were pockmarks and small caves in its melancholy surface and these were filled with clay in places, others tenanted by bugs. There were fat gray bugs that came out of the concrete and rolled into balls and almost microscopic ones with racing-yacht lines.

I phoned the fireman.

"Oh," he said, "it's you."

"Yes."

He coughed. "Well, I can't think what to do next." He added in a high voice, "You know, you do what you can, and then there's nothing left."

"Things are oozing and crawling out of this rock," I said. "You could at least have used a clean rock."

"Well."

Something in his voice disarmed me. I thought back to the days when he rattled up the driveway in his pickup truck and rushed in and grappled with that floor, untiring, humorous and hopeful.

"I swear," he said, "I wish it was my own bathroom and not yours."

We said goodbye and I've not laid eyes on him since, except now and then when I pass the firehouse and he waves as if his arm is injured and kind of looks up through his eyebrows. I never see him playing checkers with the other firemen and I have wondered if it is because the board reminds him of us.

See
the Campers
'Round
the Wretched Fire

WE LIE IN CANVAS SLING CHAIRS AND WATCH THE CARS
whiz by. The reason we are always watching cars whiz
by, and surely it must have occurred to you by now that
we do a lot of this, is because we live on the side of the
road that goes from New Orleans to Washington. I do
not know if this proves anything, but the cars headed
north from New Orleans carry people with larger and
grayer circles under their eyes than the cars going south.
Each time a car passes loaded with camping equipment

Kim leans forward, holding his breath. At times he is almost paralyzed with longing for the woods.

After a time he gazes at me and says, "Mister Coleman is a fine man, isn't he?" I agree, waiting. "He takes Frankie and Woodie camping all the time. And you know what? They all three can walk on their hands."

Kim cares nothing for continuity in his conversation. He hitches ideas together whether they fit or not. I didn't see what the hand-walking had to do with camping, but from bitter experience did not ask. Kim's explanations are by far more complex and nerve-wracking than his original statements and it was quite possible that if I stimulated him to additional words he would bring up again the business about Adam and Eve looking like baboons. Ever since the day he helped me in the yard this had been a favorite topic of Kim's and he kept showing me photographs of the Java Man in the textbook and saying that if the Java Man looked that much like a monkey Adam must've been little more than a ball of fur with two little monkey-eyes burning in the bush of him; and Lord knows *how* Eve looked.

But now, unexpectedly, it comes over me that I am not a red-blooded enough father for this boy. *Everybody* camps nowadays; it is not enough simply to loll in a chair and watch one's stomach grow.

"I can't stand on my hands," I say to Kim, "but I *can* go camping."

"You're kidding."

I take a deep breath, trying not to recall certain memories, the worst of which had to do with an evening as a Tenderfoot Scout when I dug a hole in the ground and cooked rice pudding, then stepped in it barefoot. I say to

Kim, "No, I mean it, if we can sell the rest of the family on it, I'll give her a try."

On a smoking hot afternoon three weeks later and three miles from our chosen campsite the car's left-hind tire blows and I pull over.

Mary and Mary, Jr., the latter home for a rest from nursing school, sit deadpan in the car after the tire blows. The rest of us climb out and commence unpacking the trunk to get to the spare and the tools. Some kind of a bird is yelping in the woods. It sounds as if it has swallowed a bone. Another bird says anonymously and without feeling: chew-chew-*chew;* and then, chew-choo-*chee.*

I take from the trunk my new Iglood water can, a patented cake of fly-killer, two baseball gloves and the new Safari Electrical Lantern. The equipment fascinates me. I read the stuff on the side of the lantern, which is guaranteed to throw a beam 3,000 feet. It exhilarates me to consider that by flicking a button I can punch such a hole through the darkness. Finally it is all stacked in the weeds and I am soaked with sweat as I change the tire, helped by Kim, who is also infatuated with the welter of camping gadgets; and as we work we talk happily about them. I wonder aloud how we ever managed to get along without an ice-chest made of plastic foam. Kim says he doesn't know, but that we'll never be without one again. He says that in George Martin's *Modern Camping Guide* the author states, "Modern camping may be defined as living out of doors in comfort comparable to that of a permanent home, in sleeping well-protected from the elements, and in enjoying a well-balanced, nutritious diet."

If only we had known.

Jecca reveals an unexpected aptitude for repacking

the trunk and Chris helps with small items like Mentholatum, Scotch tape and badminton birds. The four of us form what may be described as the family camping bloc. We find when the trunk is refilled that we've neglected to replace the blown-out tire. We locate twine and manage to lash the tire to the roof. Neither Mary nor Mary, Jr., offer any comment as we thump around over their heads. Mary, Jr., is reading *The Golden Scalpel.* She wears shorts of gas-flame blue and her chin is propped on bare knees. Her mother is reading *A Choice of Murders.* They seem totally uninterested in the still joys of the forest. Mary, Jr., says suddenly, "I didn't know there were *two* ways to perform a hysterectomy." Her pale eyes come alive. Any kind of surgery excites her, the bloodier the better. "There is the *regular* kind and the kind that leaves no scar and costs more."

As the camping bloc wedges back into the car Kim asks what is a hysterectomy. None of his merit badges covers this area.

We ignore him.

The public campsite is all I could have hoped for— thick woodland dappled with sunlight, a fine clearing for the tents. "This air!" I inhale. "We'll eat like horses."

My wife closes her book and looks around: "You already eat like horses. Only a *horse* could eat more like horses."

Kim supervises the pitching of the tents, issuing clear, intelligent orders to those assigned to help him. The tents are small and stand in line four feet apart, two cots to each. The women, led by Jecca, make the beds. My chest hurts from blowing up air mattresses and I stroll under the pines, surveying the situation and the terrain. It appears that tonight we will be the only campers here but our tents are pitched only a couple of hundred yards beyond the farthermost outpost of a Boy Scout encampment known as Tiak. Now and then we hear hoarse faraway cries. Perhaps someone has learned a different way to make fire, or discovered a brand new knot.

It is getting dusk and the bugs begin their evening buzzing and the pines tremble in a fresh wind. One insect, louder than the others, seems to be issuing orders from the roof of a gruesome stall made of split logs.

Even from the outside this structure lacks charm, but inside it is dark and spiderwebbed, like something in a horror movie. This is our campers' bathroom and by comparison it makes the troublesome one at home seem sinfully luxurious, practically exotic. When Mary and Mary, Jr., see it their faces go white. Hinged rectangular wooden flaps cover three holes in a splintered plank and my wife lifted a flap and gasped as if she were staring into the very depths of hell.

Later, the sky darkening, my wife looks around anxiously. "We'll eat pimento cheese—we won't cook until tomorrow. We want to be in the tents with the lights on when it's dark."

Jecca, dripping insect repellent, tries to pick up a small chromed flashlight from her cot. It gets away from her. "It just *leaked* out of my hand," she giggles. "Maybe we can do this every summer." She and Chris sparkle with pleasure, cheeks stained with fresh air and exercise. Kim is on the edge of the clearing, chopping wood, *ker-whock-kerwhock,* happy with his ax and simple, wholesome responsibilities.

§ *108* §

With the onset of darkness, a great loneliness settles over me as we sit around the fire chewing pimento cheese and bread.

Something the size of a pack rat shoots across the rosy area in the firelight. Strange night sounds come from tree and bush. *Ooga-ooo-gah.* Like an old Hupmobile horn. We stare at one another, the noises are fiercely hungry. I am acutely aware that everything in the woods, as soon as the lights are out, runs around trying to gobble up everything else little enough to kill and swallow. I wonder how many pairs of unseen eyes are on Chris, hungering for this bite-size camper.

The faint sound of cheering comes from Camp Tiak. Kim, who is an alumnus of Tiak, says, "They probably got chocolate pudding for dessert."

The mosquitoes strafe in clouds, twice the size of town mosquitoes. They are so large that when they come in for a landing the wind from their wings cools a little circle of skin. Mary, Jr., suddenly slaps at her head, "They're trying to get in my ears." Ever since I can remember she has believed that the bugs of the world desire to explore the insides of her ears.

It is very early when we go to bed, but at 10, when Taps is blown at Tiak, I am still awake. I am propped up on one elbow when I see a large humpbacked shadow thump past our tent no more than three feet from my head. Whatever it is, it's more than a foot high and I know that it has fur on it and teeth. It was no longer a simple matter of bugs and birds, the really big fellows were coming out now, the fang-and-claw boys, the ones that bit for keeps.

My wife in the cot next to me murmurs, apparently

recalling my camping sales talk of several weeks past, "Little creatures of the woods, eh?"

Mary, Jr., screams from her tent. I leap out and beam the light down the row of tents. She is sitting up, her face lotion gleaming white. "Something ran over my stomach," she says. "I'm going to get in the car and stay there until it's time to go home." She shudders and snatches up her pillow and quilt and flashlight. The car door whumps and I hear her flapping around trying to get comfortable. Minutes later Jecca follows suit; she doesn't want to be alone in a tent where a Thing ran over her sister's stomach.

I lie down again, my own stomach feeling soft and vulnerable in the night. I wonder where Kim left the short-handled ax, a wondrously sharp instrument of the latest make, forged all in one piece so that it cannot be broken. We are two miles from the highway and a mile from the heart of Tiak. I imagine a wandering psycho-path drooling over the patented ax, hefting it for weight and balance.

"Kim," I hiss, "where did you leave the ax?"

He is asleep.

My wife whispers, "It's probably out there in the dark. Anyone could kill us in our beds."

I begin pulling on my shoes. Something wriggles in one of the loafers and I rip it off. A black furred spider, limping and huge, comes out. His eyes spark redly in the light of the lantern and he does a couple of deep-knee bends, testing. My wife in a single motion evacuates her cot and runs for the car, dragging her bedding. She calls for me to bring Chris to her and when I hand him in through the window she says to wake up Kim and get him in the car, too.

"I mean this *minute*," she says in a voice she uses two or three times a year.

After leading Kim to the car I set out to find the ax. It is sticking in one of the benches near the fire, which is about dead, blue flames licking along one thin horizontal branch, skipping and jumping like the hands of a ghostly pianist. I take the ax to Kim's empty tent, locate the scabbard, and use the belt from my pants to strap it around me. I am quite a sight with the hatchet strapped over my Father's Day pajamas; the pajamas have a row of three medals printed on the chest, military-looking medals, one of them the shape and color of the Congressional Medal of Honor; and even though they are a gag and a family joke I'm rather proud of them.

Congressional Medal of Honor or not, I climb into the car.

Damned if I'm going to lie out there all alone.

My wife chuckles. "Don't tell me the Compleat Camper is going to squat here with us cravens and let all that fresh air out there go to waste?"

"I want to think a while," I answer stiffly.

That sends her and Mary, Jr., into storms of snickers. They cover their mouths and the laughter comes from their noses. In the rear-vision mirror I see white strips hanging out of Mary, Jr.'s, ears. She has torn up rags to plug out the bugs.

With the car windows up it's suffocating and smells of gasoline and grease and with the windows down the bugs flow in currents, tickling, chewing, burning, climbing the strings to Mary Jr.'s, sealed ears.

Finally I doze beneath the wheel and dream that my family is stripping the painted signs of courage from the chest of my pajamas. Jecca tells me calmly that I am a

coward and that Chris probably gets his yellow streak from me and that from this night forward I must wear plain pajamas. "It was all a mis-take," says the dream-Jecca. "We should have never got-ten the medals for you." I awaken with a jerk. I am so tired the ax digging into my kidney does not bother me enough to take it off.

Around 5:30 A.M. when the mosquitoes knock off and the horseflies and wasps take over for the day shift, I am trying to open some canned heat to start break-fast.

Kim gets up and joins me and says it's against the rules for a real woodsman to use canned heat. The can won't open anyhow. I try prying with a car key, the one to the trunk, and the key breaks off like peppermint stick. Kim rolls back on his heels and guffaws in his forthright, honest way. Something has stung him on the left nipple during the night and now it is saucy and tip-tilted, almost voluptuous. He pays it no heed and it does not interfere with his enjoyment of the moment. He does not sober down until I use his new ax to force open the car trunk so I can get at the food. "We ought to take better care of our tools," he says gravely.

The heat of the coffee melts the wax from the insides of our paper cups, but we drink it with appetite and breakfast gives us heart. We even laugh and joke a bit about the night before and we are fairly frisky through-out the day. Chris and Jecca run around the clearing hollering and they make up a game which involves the kissing of pine trees. This blackens their chins with resin and they find it hilarious. They sing a thing about "Teacher, teacher, don't be dumb—give me back my bubble gum." And another one which is even less complex, "Mother, dear, I'd love a beer, I'd *love* a beer, Mother dear."

I wait for my wife to say something about leaving for home but she doesn't. We have an excellent lunch, although the steaks seem terribly bloody on the grill in sunlight. We prowl the campsite, take naps, read and drink Cokes from the ice chest. This is more like it, the outdoor life, I keep telling myself. It is a point of honor that I am not the first one to suggest going back to town.

As the day wears on we become quieter and quieter. Soon it will be nighttime and somehow last night's alarums aren't comical any more. By twilight we eat a supper of beans and slippery wieners and we are drenched with insect repellent so that the food tastes and smells of lemon rind. All of us wear long pants and long-sleeved shirts, no pajamas this time.

If anything, this night is less desirable than the one before, alive with slithering and the chilling *Ooo-oo-gahs.*

Up and down the tent row there is the characteristic insect-slapping I now associate with a family enjoying itself on a camping trip. It occurs to me that rattlesnakes are nocturnal hunters, that they grow to six and seven feet in these regions and that one of them could coil up and bite you squarely between the eyes while you sleep. A snake of such length would not even have to get in bed with you. It is doubtful you would awaken at all, certainly not for any length of time.

I say to my wife, "Rattlesnakes and moccasins hunt at night." I control the tones, keeping them low and conversational.

"Snakes?"

"Yes."

§ *1 1 4* §

"You don't think any of them are hunting around here, do you?"

"Of course not."

She says, "I read that snakes strike anything that's warm. If there are two things that are warm they strike the warmer of the two."

"Oh?" This is not good news because I am usually much warmer than my wife. In the summertime I have only to contemplate exercise and I break out in a sweat. I am not saying that if a diamondback were coiled between the two cots I would want it to choose to sink its fangs in my wife, but at the same time I do not relish the notion that the snake would *automatically* bite me, on no more grounds than my body-temperature, a thing over which I have no control and cannot be blamed for.

Hastily I review the situation. My wife and kids are here to please me and Kim and only for that. They are enduring discomfort and possible even danger without complaint—well, without much complaint. I am *responsible* for all of them; their welfare is in my hands, a burden which must be faced.

I slap at the sharp sting of a mosquito and at the sound something scuttles between the tents. I reach out and touch my wife and she lurches upright. "My God," she says, "don't *grab* me like that."

"Get up," I say, "we're going home."

There is a small halo of bugs around her head as I flash the lantern on her. "Thank God," she says. She kisses me for the first time since we left home.

I move along the line of tents, routing them out with the word that we are leaving. We are heading for home, for soap and steaming water and roast beef and gravy.

"Everybody up!" They smile worshipfully at me. There is excited talk in the tents as they gather clothing, equipment and provisions. Mary, Jr., says now she will be able to keep her date with George, who always buys her a cheeseburger at the Frost Top before bringing her home. Jecca says we will be home in time for "Twilight Zone."

And when the tents are struck, in the final moments before leaving, Kim slides up with a whispered message: "Daddy, you know how the Colemans can walk on their hands? Well, you know, they fall down a lot."

I don't know if it was the truth, but it seemed an awful nice thing for Kim to say.

The Sweet
Sloppiness
of Valentine's Day

KIM AND I WERE AT THE DRUGSTORE AND I WAS FLUSHED
with relief at having finally caught up again with my
bill. A modern drug bill is something that takes some
catching up *with,* in this day of the 50-cent capsule when
a common cold can cripple a man financially and a siege
of strep throats in a large family may bankrupt the leader
of the clan. I happened to see a row of red-satin candy
boxes glimmering on a shelf. The Valentine boxes were
shaped like hearts and had stiff scarlet bows on them

and scallops of scratchy looking gold lace, all of it very new and cardboard-smelling. Yet old as the hills, achingly nostalgic.

I suggested we get a big box for his mother and a smaller one for his girl friend, but Kim (he calls his girl friend George instead of Georgiana) looked embarrassed. He said the hearts were a little corny and that a real heart wasn't shaped like that anyway; that a heart didn't have a point on one end and a dent in the other, that it was more of a glob.

Regaining composure, he propounded at length on such drab truths as the auricle and the ventricle. He said his teacher told him there wasn't anything sissy or delicate about a normal heart, that it was the ruggedest and most amazing muscle in the body and if you took care of it in the course of a lifetime it would pump hundreds of thousands of gallons of blood, enough blood to float a ship.

As I mooned at a red box and half listened to my science-age son it struck me as pathetic that modern youth appeared to be less interested in the sweet sloppiness of Valentine's Day than in the melancholy vision of a ship on a sea of blood.

Selecting a box for Mary, I harked back to the first time I ever bought a box of Valentine candy for a girl, back in the days when a heart was more than a muscle. The girl's name was Boyce Leigh Sadler and she wore her hair in long black curls of the diameter and springiness of a garden hose.

She was a toe dancer (a fact Jecca would savor but which would not impress Kim), a member of Miss Grace Finn's Dancing Academy, which annually staged a "recital" at the Saenger Theater. I would clap until there was no feeling in my hands, only a dull pain, as Boyce Leigh scissored over the waxed boards on long pearl-pale legs, caught in a golden bubble of light.

She had no idea, no way of knowing, how much I cared, even though we were in the same fourth-grade class, for I never spoke to her except once, to pick up a piece of chalk she had dropped and say, "Here." I used to love to watch her hair swing in its separate cylinders as she did long division at the blackboard. I suffered agonies when she botched a problem and if the teacher scolded her I sat there sweating, impaled, destroyed.

My best friend, Tom McLure, fancied the same girl and it galled me that his family allowed him, once each week, to wear his best suit to school. In class I liked to dream that I wore a suit superior to Tom's fine brown one and that I, whenever I wished, could float from my desk and circle the room, not making any noise, but flying easily and calmly until everyone was bug-eyed with admiration.

I dreamed, too, of swooping down to rescue Boyce Leigh from intricate masses of grinding factory-type machinery while Tom cowered helpless in his fine feathers.

I saved secretly for weeks to buy the box of Whitman's Sampler as a Valentine present, afraid Tom would find out and buy one, too. Valentine's fell on a Saturday and after breakfast I went to the garage and slid the hidden heart-shaped box from under some newspapers in a corner in the shadow of the hulking Hudson Super-Six.

Slowly I walked the seven blocks to Boyce Leigh's

house and, sick with suspense, hurled the box on the front porch and ran.

I heard a door slam and a man's voice sang out: "Come back here, come back, boy."

My legs turned to rubber and such a dizzy surge filled me I thought I was going to fall down on the sidewalk, helpless and exposed to the world; but I kept running because I knew I couldn't possibly face them after having declared my feeling for Boyce Leigh. I'd placed no card in the candy, but as I lurched crazily toward home I pictured her placing piece after piece of the rich Whitman's Sampler in her mouth and saying: "Elliott did it. He bought it for me. Nobody else could have done it."

Weeks afterward I couldn't look directly at her because of the shimmering image of her chewing my candy, such an intimate and revealing thing, almost too much to bear. She never gave a sign she knew who threw the candy and I didn't say anything. It was enough just to ponder it.

Now I paid the clerk for Mary's candy and Kim selected some comic Valentine and he and I walked back to the car. He told me some fellow had figured out how many times a human heart beat during an average lifetime, that it ran into the billions.

The Bishop's
Pomegranates

SOMEWHERE ALONG THE WAY THE TRICK-OR-TREAT
thing found a toehold among the timid and there is no
question but that it casts a beggarly pall on Halloween
night, a night that used to prickle with hairbreadth adventure. It is saddening to see perfectly healthy and
mischievous children traveling tamely from house to
house, sweating off their false mustaches in the dull
business of asking for "treats." A heartbreaking essay
could be done on the treats alone, the shattered cookie,
the ancient peanut butter kiss, the ruptured tangerine,
the molten Hershey bar, almonds adrift and worn.

§ *122* §

I grieve for the days of the treatless trick and recall climbing a white lattice fence to swipe pomegranates from his excellency the bishop's backyard tree.

The bishop, I think he was a retired one, would sit on an upstairs porch and watch us and sometimes he would thump the floor with his cane. He knew it was expected of him. He seemed to appreciate the dignity and fine danger of those Halloweens and I believe if we'd asked him he would have been pleased to come down and climb the fence with us.

The running in the dark was best of all, the bruising, giggling collisions, invisible clotheslines and near-amputations. There was the good crazy feeling of pursuit, someone or *something* pounding after you in the night. And finally you rested in the dense shadows of a tree and your buddy said: "Lordy, he nell got us that time. I declare if he didn't." You knew there had been no true chase, but the truth mattered least of all.

If you were a gutsy one you may have managed to hide the lawn furniture of the funeral home down the street. And if you truly blazed with courage you ran onto the porch and jammed a splinter in the doorbell, plunging into a bush for cover and waiting to watch the old embalmer answer the door. There he was, darkly tall and stooped, built like a coffin, sniffing the air of October and grinning horribly in his secret knowledge of the dead.

You knew he would rush out and kill you with his bare claws if he could find you. He was at least forty years old and it never occurred to you he was getting a kick out of it.

You saved the bishop's pomegranates till last, after

the goose-bumped joys of ticka-tack and the rest, because the pomegranates were the best of all, the cool soursweet pebbles against your tongue. You straddled the fence and blew the seeds at the moon and the skin tightened along your spine when you heard the hammering of the bishop's cane.

I'll never forget the taste of those pomegranates. What a pale trade for them, these modern "treats" collected in a brown paper bag.

Honestly, some of the stuff my kids bring home in bags, I can hardly eat at all.

Whatever Happened to Baby Ray?

IT IS WITH MIXED, IF NOT MANGLED, EMOTIONS, THAT I relate here the fact that Chris has commenced using with regularity the family library card.

At present he's deep in a book about a little French cat that lives in the palace of Versailles.

Chris won't let loose of this sophisticated thing throughout the day, taking it to school with him where, as I pointed out earlier, he is having his second crack at the first grade. The teacher says Chris is not stupid

§ 126 §

but that he will not listen and since all he hears is himself he gains ground rather more slowly than other children. At night he lies in bed with the book propped on his belly, legs crossed, quoting entire passages: "I am a French cat. My name is Minette . . . Monsieur Henri does not like me. I do not like Monsieur Henri."

Someone of course has to help Chris with the stranger words, but once he latches onto them they stick fast. Mary was worried for a time that perhaps it was not good for Chris to pretend day after day he was a French cat, a female French cat at that. And it really is unnerving to hear a mere pink stub of a lad give out with: "But moi, Minette, it does not amuse me to spend my time being nice to that dog lover."

I don't even know the meaning of *moi* and I'll be hanged if I'll ask him.

When Mary began taking Chris to the library and letting him browse along the tots' shelves he was for a time satisfied with things like, "Poor Jane Ray, her bird is dead, she cannot play!"

There were childish line drawings of Jane Ray not playing, and of the deceased bird, toes upturned.

Granted it was morbid, it was the kind of thing a six-year-old could be expected to grasp; and it was plain the bird hadn't died violently, that the little girl had loved it and done her best by it when it was alive; that it was a sincere (you could tell by its toes), grudgeless American bird without a thought of Versailles or Monsieur Henri, or even of the state capitol.

Minette, in contrast to Jane Ray, never talks down to her little readers. She will slip them an occasional parenthetical explanation and that only when the going is

fearfully slippery: "People come from all over the world to visit my palace. It is what we French call a *Monument Historique* (historic monument). . . ."

So much for the foreign flavor. As for the plot of this suave and fascinating book, there is complication and delicacy here, a war of nerves between Minette and Henri, who is palace caretaker, suspense built powerfully in page after page of prose and illustration; until finally this French mouse comes along.

The mouse is not a patriot like Minette and doesn't care a fig about the condition of the historic monument, chewing the tips off draperies and silken bedspreads, leaving mousetracks on the chairs. Old Henri finally gets an *historique* chewing from *Monsieur le Ministre,* who comes from Paris now and again to see if everything is all right at the palace.

Nothing, of course, is all right, what with the mouse gobbling up history as fast as it can.

In the end (I shall not hold you in thrall much longer) the French government *insists* that Minette sleep in the Royal Bed, no matter how Henri feels about it, and Minette catches the bad mouse and spanks it and tells it if it ever returns it will be her duty, as a patriot, to eat it.

Minette, relenting slightly, tells the mouse to go down the street to Dupont's Grocery where there is something better to eat than curtains. Monsieur Henri, who early in the story was busy hurling Minette outdoors, gets his comeuppance in the grand manner.

That, obviously, is plot enough for a year-long TV series, plots being what they are these days, but it isn't enough for Chris, who really is convinced at times that he is a French cat. He says that mouse has begun acting pretty much the fool down at Dupont's and sooner or later he will have to go down there and straighten things out.

Crashless
Salmon
Diet

DESPAIRING AT LAST OF ALL THE MORE POPULAR DIETS
and casting about for a workable reducing program
which would get the job done without that caved-in feeling, or the perfumed nausea of my earlier apricot kick,
I got to thinking, quite naturally, of Eskimos.

For some it is not natural to think of Eskimos but
rarely does a week pass that I don't spend at least a few
minutes musing on these gallant quick-frozen people.
I've never seen a truly fat Eskimo. In the photographs

§ *131* §

they have fat faces but when you see pictures of them stripped of furs they are pretty stringy, looking strangely small, like wet cats.

I mentioned this to Mary and told her I contemplated a diet of salmon.

She said a large percentage of Eskimos suffered from tuberculosis and probably that kept them trim; that if I planned to lose weight gobbling oily canned fish I would have to sleep out in the rain and develop a dependable respiratory ailment. Although the children found this funny, I considered it misguided humor which, in time, would trouble her conscience.

The second night of the salmon I had a feeling something was missing and sure enough, it tasted better with three or four glurps of mayonnaise.

The third night I added a pile of fresh soda-crackers and the following evening improved on this by throwing in some green onions and washing it down with a couple of Cokes. Mary said she never heard of an Eskimo guzzling Coke. I explained patiently that where they live it is too cold, the Coke would freeze and burst the bottle.

By week's end the salmon was ringed with smoking drifts of canned pork and beans, celery, green onions, crackers, triple helpings of lettuce (which is totally unfattening), the whorls of mayonnaise, potato chips and sweet pickles (pickles having practically no calories). This progressively inverted diet had whetted my appetite to such knife edge that not even the little radishes along the extreme outer edge of the plate seemed to give me indigestion.

Ordinarily radishes kill me.

And at any other time green onions are hurtful to me,

but now, in the company of the salmon, they traveled the circuit without a twinge.

The following week I remained on the salmon although it appealed less now. But I knew it was grand for my thyroid because of the iodine, and I reminded myself that my thyroid probably needed a little touching up because when I'm angry or distressed my eyes bulge.

Mary went right along with her regular cooking: red beans and rice, pork chops, cabbage and the like. I began borrowing from her routine, unimaginative dinners, throwing a chop or so onto my salmon plate. Perhaps a puff of creamed potatoes, a steaming slice of cornbread. I was not fussy about dessert and made no effort to engineer my own. Whatever the family was having was good enough for me.

I'd no desire to become a fanatic.

During eighteen days of the diet my weight failed to drop. Actually, for some reason, it soared from 226 to 234. Although I found it difficult to lace my left shoe I never felt better internally. There was no problem in lacing the right shoe and to this day that phenomenon defies medical explanation. Several times I have examined myself in the private depths of the bathroom mirror and I am no fatter on the left side than on the right.

Even Mary was intrigued by this. She said that Eskimos wore *mukluks* and scorned lacings for shoes.

It's certainly a thing to think about.

In any event I have sworn off salmon and that in itself is noteworthy, it being the first time I ever quit anything and made it stick.

You
Never
Had
a Baby

"YOU NEVER *had* A BABY," MARY SAYS TO ME. "IF YOU ever had one you'd feel different, you'd understand a *lot* of things."

I try to light the pipe she likes me to smoke, but the tobacco hisses and stinks and the coal dies. I ask her, "How many men do you know that have had a baby?"

"Oh, shut up," she says. "You know what I mean."

I drop the pipe back in the rack. "Name one, just one."

"Ah, it's no use, you're just being silly."

§ *1 3 4* §

"Did President Kennedy ever have a baby? Did Frank Sinatra? Did your Uncle Joe or Whitey Ford?" I mention several other fairly successful men who have made their mark without going into obstetrics. For years Mary has been throwing it up to me that I never had a baby and I consider the time has come to bring the thing out in the open and to establish that I am but one of millions of fathers who have failed in this area.

Generally speaking she is a reasonable woman. I don't mean she makes a fetish of being reasonable, but she is not a bore about the fact that I don't menstruate or sew.

This whole thing came up today on the tail end of a number of other things right in the middle of my trying to write a book which I've no choice to do anything *but* write because I spent the $2,000 advance for it six months ago. Quite early in the morning the Mazola spits up out of the skillet onto her forearm and raises a blister as big around and as thick as a vanilla wafer. When I tell you that you can actually hear the water sloshing around inside this blister I am not lying, and I have to stick a hole in the transparent skin of the blister-bag and drain it, after first sterilizing the needle, which is so short it gets hot all over when I hold a match under the point.

This takes time. Just *finding* a needle in this house takes time, believe me. The morning is shot by the time she is satisfied that I have drained the bag as flat as it will go and I have not produced five lines of any kind of writing. I must then go to the drugstore for *Foille* and bandages and return and apply them so that she is well enough protected to prepare lunch. I am very hungry since she did not serve much of a breakfast after cooking her arm.

Jecca comes home at noon with a wooden splinter under the nail of her middle finger. "I just went to pick up my books off the gym floor," she says. "It's killing me."

She cries quietly and screams when her mother tries to dig out the splinter with a needle. Yes, the same needle. Jecca, it develops, has not been screaming at all, because when her mother gets the tweezers under that nail Jecca demonstrates the real thing, a fullthroated howl that lifts me by the nape of the neck. I am sitting at the typewriter. Nothing is what I've written and nothing is what I am going to write this day.

Jecca comes to me, red-eyed and howling. Her mother follows her, bandaged, burned and shaken, and hands me the needle. "Here, you try, I can't do anything with it."

The tweezers are blunt as pliers and I spend precious minutes looking for a file. I have not eaten and the work is at a standstill. A week ago I quit my newspaper job to write this book and since that time the interruptions have been practically constant, so that the few pages I *have* completed are of a caliber which, by contrast, makes now-is-the-time-for-all-good-men sound like Nobel Prize material. I must sharpen the tweezers on the whetstone in the kitchen and by then we are into the afternoon; not just any old afternoon, but the afternoon that my wife breaks her tooth on a banana kiss while watching *West Side Story* downtown at the Saenger. She isn't gone from the house an hour.

I am asleep, hoping to knit my nerves and energy sufficiently to resume writing. Mary slaps me on the leg and when I awake she is kneeling beside the bed, her cheek pulled back so that I can see the broken tooth. It is a sight to turn the blood to water. She is weeping quietly. I groan and roll over and study the ceiling. What does she want of me now? It is too much. I have never extracted an adult tooth, my only experience having been with Chris, and you simply pinch out his little teeth with a piece of Kleenex.

Suddenly Mary brightens and smiles and lets loose of her cheek. "I just wanted you to see it; I feel better now." The bandage on her burned arm is moist from tears. At any rate we are gaining ground since two things have been fixed, the blister and Jecca's splinter and only one new crisis has arisen. I get up and sit down at the little typewriter table in the bedroom and spend five minutes reading the words Smith-Corona on the machine. My mind is dead. It threatens to bog in the middle of Smith, stumbles across the hyphen and gradually absorbs Corona, swallowing it strenuously, the way a python engulfs a pig. My wife says there has been no letter from Bill in three weeks, nor has he phoned. I say sluggishly, my head gorged with Smith-Corona and disaster, "Fine, that's fine."

"What do you mean?" says Mary.

"—you'll hear from him, he's busy, he's got his hands full."

"I worry so about him," she says. "You hardly ever even mention his name."

In my state I am no match for her. The two operations and the jolt of the broken tooth coated with banana kiss have taken their toll. For the life of me I cannot remember the last time I mentioned Bill's name.

"You know I love Bill," I say.

"But he's my *baby*," she says. "You never had a baby, you don't know what it's like. He's my flesh and blood."

"Well, he's my, ah—*son*." I find myself reacting in the usual way, feeling apologetic. This has been going on for a long, long time, yet not until now do I arrive at the perfect defense. I lay the cards on the line and *admit* the shortcoming. It's the only way. It's no good trying to pretend.

Sonic-Boom
Lips

UNTIL THIS SONIC-BOOM THING STARTED I NEVER SAW
my wife with one lip white and one red.

Last Friday afternoon I went to town to buy some
paper and carbon sheets and when I came home her
upper lip was quite naked. She said she didn't get around
to painting it because as she stood before the mirror
there was this tremendous thump that rattled the whole
house. In a little while there was another gumbling
whump and a picture swung sideways on the wall. "My

§ *139* §

mascara box was on the dresser and the little hard brush in the box began chattering like a squirrel."

She said after the first thump all her thinking processes slowed to a creep, but her heart began racing. And finally, when the heart resumed its normal beat, she went out on the back porch and looked up at the sky through the bare branches of the mulberry tree to try to see the plane. Her chest ached slightly. A colored maid was shaking a rug on the Joneses' porch. "She looked so ordinary and sensible it reassured me."

I tried to explain, casually, what puts the pow in a sonic boom, but I never can remember clearly what I've read about things like that and I saw that my fumbling was making her more nervous, not calming her as I'd hoped to do. And further, her lips confused me, the painted lip appearing uncommonly heavy and the other floating weightless and lost above it. It emphasized the enormity of the force which had caused her to quit painting at the halfway mark.

I've seen her apply lipstick, flawlessly, while racked with labor pains as we waited for a taxi to take us to the hospital in New Orleans.

And I've known her to do a fair to middling paint job in the early stages of a hurricane while garbage can tops whanged off the roof like big birds and the house shivered like a live thing as Lake Pontchartrain heaved up into our yard and floated beer cans from under all the gray asbestos duplexes.

She can paint her mouth without smearing at sixty miles an hour on a bumpy road. Nor does her hand falter in the black of night, nor in rain or sleet, nor amidst the screams of large and angry children cursing one another and milling outside the bathroom door, readying themselves to worship the Lord on a Sabbath morning.

Remembering these and other instances of her courage and skill with a tube of lipstick I did not laugh at her now.

"I wish," she said, "they would leave the sound barrier alone or go break it somewhere else."

She said until they started bashing it, everything was fine; that she didn't even know it was being broken until one summer when she was visiting her mother in Louisiana. There was something wrong with the brakes of the car and she took it to a garage. "I asked the man how much it would cost and as he was telling me there was this hasty boom and the handle of his jack began rattling and lifting up and down *obscenely*."

She said she walked back to her mother's place and later in the day the man phoned and said the car was ready, to come pick it up. "It cost $50 and I couldn't complain because he said he'd told me it might. He said they had to grind down all the brake drums, whatever they are."

She says that now whenever she hears a sonic boom, or practically any kind of boom, she remembers with horror how she felt when the garage man said $50, "He asked for the money as casually as you'd ask a friend for a cigarette."

She's convinced that if no one had ever smashed the sound barrier she would have been able to hear the man in the beginning and could have shopped around and got the brakes fixed for a fraction of the price. She finds no consolation in the fact that her mother gave her the money, plus a little extra for Chris's tetanus shots after he stabbed himself in the face with a rusty toy truck.

Now she pursed contrasty lips and said in hollow, fatigued tones, "When people start rushing around breaking the very air we breathe, no one is safe."

And, who's to deny it?

Dignity
of Mankind
—Hoo-Boy!

EVERYWHERE YOU TURN THESE DAYS THERE IS TALK about the innate dignity of mankind and this is pretty peculiar because almost any second-rate mongrel dog trotting down the street in a veil of gnats has more genuine dignity in the stub of his tail than the United States Senate and House combined, and them wearing tails too, or golden mail, for that matter. Man simply is not a dignified animal and his children are even less so and it is a fact we should learn to live with, not in the name of self-criticism, or masochism, but simply accept it, so that our current literature and television programs may move on to things of more genuine interest.

Once we accept the truth that an adult man is for the most part a simpering, politicking opportunist who tramples his inferiors (one way or another; he may even trample them with kindness and exaggerated thoughtfulness) and that almost all children are recurrently repulsive, then and then only will we cast off the fetters that cloud the pages of our books and louse up the TV screen.

A repulsive child can be fascinating, and a superficial or affected adult is not without interest. It is when the author or the playwright must devote a third of his lineage to the losing proposition of dignity that the game is up.

It can get pretty funny, but not funny in the way that is liable to keep you awake for any length of time. On one extremely popular TV program there is this little kid with a golden heart who is always making childish mistakes like poisoning the family horse. When the family horse recovers and gets up and shakes itself, still sick as hell, mind you, but able to struggle up off the ground, the kid's mother and father exchange long, grateful, quivering glances. They stare lovingly at the kid, getting across the idea that he has become a bigger and more dignified person through the medium of poisoning the horse. The kid has *learned* something. He has learned that strychnine will just about flatten the family pet, and that is *all* the little bastard has learned, if you ask me. But the TV parents don't see it this way, and minutes are wasted as the camera dwells on the two large philosophic faces and the mean little face. In the time it takes to establish the point that there is a world of dignity in a bottle of strychnine the kid could have poisoned a whole herd of horses *and* his mother and father, which would pep things up and necessitate a brand-new mother and father, an element this show has needed for years. Better yet, the kid could run offstage and poison the writer.

No one ever whales the kid with a limber peachtree switch. This would raise a welt on his dignity.

Further, it would diminish the dignity of the father and mother, who, it must be said, have perfected the time-consuming soulful stares to such degree there is little else left of the show; and if you jettisoned the business of the eyeballs where would you be? I'll tell you where you would be. You would be enjoying a decent nap and not sitting there waiting for something sensible to happen that never does.

There is another show, a western-type one, where the little kid (another kid) gets his old man out of all kinds of scrapes, teaches him the true meaning of dignity and living, saves his life, cheers him up, cues him on how to act around women.

Now, the cowboy-farmer father is more than six feet tall and he can handle a carbine like a Thompson submachine gun, and he is quiet-spoken and reflective and has the courage of a Kamikaze pilot. But that isn't enough. When things get truly rugged he seeks the counsel of the nipper. No matter what the kid docs, it enlarges both his personality and that of the man. Once the kid was messing around in a forbidden old mine tunnel and a pile of rocks fell on him. His dad had told him to stay out of there, but all that was forgotten and when Dad had excavated the little joker you were compelled to watch them mooning at each other until the sponsors were convinced you had absorbed the lesson. The man, of course, could have been squashed flat as a wallet in that tunnel trying to save the disobedient little brat. But who cares?

I care. I've tried not to, but I care.

When the TV people feel the camera isn't adequate for the weight of the message, they allow the actors to come right out and say the words: "the dignity of mankind." Even on Bonanza, which I enjoy much of the time, there is loose talk of dignity. I don't know how many cows those fellows own or how many times a week their lives are in peril, or how often they have to help someone out of a hopeless situation in every conceivable kind of weather, they still find time to talk about dignity. Ordinarily, though, they don't allow it to interfere with the action; they just spit it out and jump on a quarter-horse and hammer on down the canyon to locate Little Joe's half-brother, who is kind of a murderer.

If you listen too intently to the script and you don't keep a watch on yourself these days, you find yourself losing perspective. The Mexicans have dug a hole and buried a man up to his chin in the broiling sun and the ants are busy. You are less worried about the ants getting in the poor devil's nose than you are about his dignity.

He said only a minute before they planted him that he would die well, he would go out with dignity intact. I mean, after all, if *he* wasn't especially concerned about those ants you are likely to shrug them off too. It is not a wholesome thing, this ignoring *everything* in the interests of human nobility. And in real life the man in the hole wouldn't care two cents about how he behaved so long as he could raise enough fuss to get out of there and go on home and get a bath.

A retired gunman who has lost his speed and most of his nerve gets his gun out of hock when the new champ challenges him. The retired gunsel is heavy on the juice because his fiancée, who had long blond curls, was scalped by the Sioux. Admittedly it is enough to make a man drink excessively if he is an admirer of blond hair; but this man has been stoned for a year and his gun hand shakes badly as he readies himself for death in the street. Someone asks him why he insists on tangling with a younger, faster gun when the fatal outcome is obvious.

"My dignity," says the idiot. "It's all I've got left."

Yet he didn't have enough dignity to keep from getting smashed on weekdays, Sundays and even Christmas.

It is confusing as well as corrupting.

Primarily because dignity invariably is related to the death of a man or beast, or the near-death, as in the case of the brat who fed the family horse that stuff.

I don't want my kids growing up to believe they've got to get knocked off to be dignified. In fact, and this is the truth if I ever told it, I don't want them growing up thinking that it's either practical, or *possible* to be dignified.

Chris, of all our children, appears to be the least plagued by aspirations to dignity, and this is not altogether a matter of acute youth with him, it is more a forthright willingness to admit there are phases of life which by their very texture and design are meant to intimidate.

He is in a state of perpetual intimidation—by the

German police dog down the street, by spinach, a hard-fisted five-year-old in the next block, by skeletons.

Right now it is the skeletons.

A while ago he came in and told me he saw a skeleton dancing in the dining room. At first I thought he was referring to one of Jecca's ballet friends, because there is one of an extreme transparency whose movements and appearance are oddly meatless. More of meat later; that is, of meat as it is related to bones.

"You're kidding me," I said. "It's a joke, a little joke *between* us."

"No," Chris said, "it was dancing in there in the dark, standing straight up and it had teeth like butcher-knives; if you came close it would *eat* you."

Many of these lovely images he collects from his sister Jecca, who knows better, but who pinches him in the middle of murder movies and who delights in shrieking into his small ear at the worst times possible. As much as she loves sweets, and she is a regular chocolate-termite, if given her choice between an unblemished devil's food cake and the opportunity to goad Chris into a clammy sweat, she would elect the latter, even if she were verging on starvation. I asked him now if Jecca had been telling him stories. Skeleton stories.

"Yes," he said. "Skeletons are bones, we got them in our heads."

This assuredly had the Jecca touch. Apparently she planned to make the terror an inescapable one, to set it up so that the child would live in fear of his own skull.

"They can't hurt you, son. Skeletons are dead. I mean the ones without anything *on* them are dead."

§ *148* §

"Meat? You mean without any meat?"

I flinched.

"What's worse than a skeleton is a munster," he said, hair swirling excitedly, like yellow smoke. "A munster will bite anything that moves. It will kill anything big enough to die. It can jump out from under a bridge and bite a billy goat in two."

"There's no such thing as that kind of monster."

"Jecca *said*."

"She was joking, to make you laugh."

"Well, it don't make me laugh," he sighed. I took him to his room and put him back into bed and said: "Pull up your cover now, it's time to go to sleep. I'll turn out the light."

"I'm scared."

"There's nothing to be scared of; I told you skeletons are dead and monsters don't even exist, not the kind you're talking about."

"What kind they *got*?" He has this knack for cutting away the fluff and getting down to essentials.

"Now, look, that's enough, go to sleep."

"What's that noise?"

"It's cats, under the house." I patted the side of his head, which was sweating lightly.

He popped bolt upright. "It's a skeleton."

I called for Jecca and after the usual interval of waiting she appeared in the doorway, blonde and studiedly placid, her lids shining characteristically. For some reason she has oily lids and frequently wears them at half-mast to demonstrate them. "You tell Chris this minute there is no skeleton in the dining room or anywhere else."

"That would be a lie," she said, her lids shimmering.

"All right, tell him that nothing is going to bother him—ah, that the Lord looks after little boys who say their prayers and behave."

"He never says his prayers," she observed coldly, looking at him in such a way that he is forever accused and damned.

"Explain to him you were joking."

"I was joking," she said flatly.

"No you weren't." His clear small voice quavered. "They're under the *planks*."

She assumed the bored look, one of her best. She can convey a boredom so complete and excruciating that it curls the gray toes of her sneakers. "Those are *cat* skeletons under the floor, little bro-ther."

"What?"

"And the cats are wearing them—that's not the kind you have to wor-ry about."

It was getting out of hand and if there was any dignity remaining in the room Jecca had all of it, a complete monopoly. The lot of it, transient as it was, and cruel. Chris flopped against the pillow, spent. He seemed to appreciate what I'd tried to do for him. He blinked as if in apology at having caused so much trouble. He said: "I didn't see one like I said dancing in the dining room."

"Fine, that's fine, son, always tell the truth."

"It was just standing there, not dancing at all." Chris yawned. "But it had these teeth that could bite clear through your chest."

With a fellow like this on the premises, who *needs* television? I am thankful, too, that he never poisons

§ *151* §

horses or tries to help me in my moments of pain or worry. Last year either he or his pal Wellington sat fatally on a live rabbit next door, but the rabbit was left over from Easter and was practically worn out anyhow.

Accident
in Masculinity

JECCA FINALLY TOOK THE BIT IN HER TEETH AND SAID she was going to make a man of Chris; that she was sick of seeing him run every time somebody said scat. "Why," she said, "he's yellow as a—he's yellow as a *school bus.*"

After about a week of Jecca's Chris-toughening program it became apparent that Chris remained about the same but that Jecca was becoming markedly manly, clumping around the house as if she wore army boots, swaggering, speaking with a hoarse emphasis. Her blue

§ *153* §

gaze became disturbingly direct and not even her laugh was the way it used to be.

Each night she insisted that Chris punch a pillow and growl. It seemed to bore him but he went through with it so she would shut up and leave him alone. "You are a tough lit-tle boy," she said to him as he slugged the pillow. "A ver-ry tough lit-tle boy, you *hear?*" Or, she might say: "You are not going to run from John any more, you are not going to be a sissy, you *hear?*" Chris didn't bother to answer because he knew perfectly well that if John came after him he was going to make as many tracks as possible before the attack materialized. He was going to give John every chance in the world not to catch him. John is the same age as Chris, the son of a car salesman who lives down the street. A fleet black-eyed child, John thus far had never failed to overhaul Chris, but giving credit where it is due, Chris always went down sprinting.

Jecca, who is a born mimic, leaned heavily on this talent in her training of Chris, aping the swashbuckling movements of teen-age boys whenever she was in the company of her little brother. In the beginning it was a deliberate act with her, but as time passed and the groove deepened the exception became the rule and she would stand with one hip cocked out like the late James Dean and chest hollowed in the Kazan slouch, or crouch, or whatever it is. In blue jeans she was a very arresting-looking fellow. We didn't interfere because Chris does have a rather blotterlike personality and we hoped he would soak up some of Jecca's brave posturing.

He remained firmly yellow into the second week.

And the third.

In the fourth week it was observed he could no longer

pretend to be even slightly angry at the pillow and he declined to punch it any more. When Jecca waggled the pillow and hissed at him and told him he was tough, he simply sighed and went into his room and lay down, shading his eyes with the backs of his hands, refusing to look at her. He no longer followed her around as in the old days, and you got the impression she embarrassed him. There was no question but that he preferred her in the feminine condition.

One afternoon I heard snarling out front and from the door saw Jecca engaged in a fistfight with an older girl who lives in the next block. Jecca shuffled and danced beneath the camphor tree, at intervals flicking out a left, then feinting and striking the girl in the stomach with a solid right. You would have thought she'd been mixing it up all her life. The larger child was giving as good as she got, but her movements were awkward and ladylike and she racked up points by slapping Jecca on top the head and clawing her cheeks until Jecca's eyes watered.

Chris quailed against the trunk of the tree. Now and then he stiffened and said weakly: "Git her, Jeck, git her in the belly." Then he would glance back over his shoulder to make certain John was nowhere in sight. This backward glance had become a conditioned reflex and no matter what Chris was doing he managed a periodic examination of the terrain and the situation.

Now Jecca's antagonist made a darting movement toward Chris and he swung swiftly around the tree, placing the trunk of it where it would do the most good.

Jecca intercepted the girl as I grabbed them both. "She called Chris a *sissy*," Jecca panted. Then she pulled away from me, wheeled and snarled at Chris, who

clutched the trunk of the camphor, "You're a tough lit-tle boy, you *hear?*"

"Yes," he said, not letting go of the tree.

The following day two extraordinary things happened: Jecca went back to being a girl, and Chris won a clear-cut victory over John Connelly, a triumph all the sweeter because it was so long in coming, dazzling against a sustained and somber background of defeat, small quantities of blood and tubs of tears.

John and his police dog, the latter large as a calf, leaped out from behind the Traubs' azalea bush next door.

Chris, I am told by Mrs. Traub, clenched his fists and said to John: "Are you going to be *nice* today?"

"No," said John, who is not a liar.

Upon hearing this, Chris pivoted and sped for home beating John to the front door by a good five paces and slamming the door in John's face.

Orange
Vomit

CHRIS SAYS, "LOOK A THERE, THERE'S TEDDY—YOU RE-
member Teddy don't you, he's the little boy that vomited
on the picnic, *orange* vomit."

I am driving Chris home from school and he is clutching the dashboard. He is not content unless he is leaving
his fingerprints on something. This is as important to
him as oxygen. I am convinced he would turn black in
the face and fall senseless if he were forced to go five
minutes without touching a thing. He even sleeps holding something. It doesn't matter what: an empty bottle

of paste, a cracker-box, a broken candle. "Hi Teddy," Chris calls out the window.

Teddy Wellington, who vomited orange on the picnic, does not answer. He is having trouble, several kinds of trouble at once. He is wearing skunk mittens, which are very big this year at Camp Elementary School. These are black items of cotton fiber with white stripes down the middle and white flannel tails hanging from the tips of the finger places. Teddy's sweater is half on and he is trying to push a skunk mitten through the dangling right sleeve and at the same time hang onto his books. He wears very thick tinted spectacles and looks as tame as lamb chops. You would not think that once he and Chris sat on a rabbit. Or that they buried a little girl's lunch money behind the school. Chris maybe, but not Teddy; you wouldn't figure Teddy for any kind of foolishness.

"Miz Miley says Teddy's the only boy that ever did that on the picnic," Chris says, squeezing and unsqueezing and squeezing the dashboard. "She said it was too many pops."

"He's famous?"

"Yes," says Chris.

"On account of that?"

"Yes."

"You must be hurting for heroes at school."

"Also he clawed Claude, he clawed Claude *up*."

"Oh."

"Claude don't mess with Teddy no more—two times, like a wild animal," says Chris. "Teddy don't hit, he grabs them in the middle of the face. If Claude was water you couldn't *pour* him on Teddy."

Children are strung out along the street from Camp

School. Most of them are little and loud but there are the sad ones, the scared ones, and looking at them you remember that grammar school was not altogether a bucketful of honeysuckle.

"That's Karina," says Chris. "I kissed her."

"Did she like it?"

"No," he says.

"How come?"

"I don't know, but *I* liked it. I like to kiss."

"It's very good," I agree. "Watch out, you're going to fall out the window."

Chris says, "Hi Karina."

She nods faintly. She has heavy blond hair that jumps. She is maybe eight, two years older than Chris. "Hi," he says, clutching the window ledge and leering. "Man, she can *hit*," he says. "She can hit like a *mule*."

"Hi, Clancy," says Chris. Clancy ignores him, intent on a yo-yo that appears to be perforated and chromed and rusted. The yo-yo falls, sucks up the string and shoots out straight and swings. "He squirts the hose in his swim shorts," says Chris. "Once I went over to play with him and he was out in the yard with the hose and all he did was stand around and squirt it down inside his swim trunks; he said it made him feel funny."

"Did you try it?"

"I didn't have on no trunks."

"Did you *try* it?"

"Yes," he sighs. "It tickled."

He climbs into the back of the car and begins swaying from side to side, bending his knees, half-standing. The leather button on his cap goes tick-tock against the ceiling. He holds onto the back of the front seat with one hand and braces the other against the dome light. "Dean, hey Dean!" Dean is oblivious. He is aboard an outgrown bicycle and looks like a chimpanzee assaulting a roller skate. Dean is small but the bike is smaller, with wheels the size of dinner plates. "He's in my Sunday school," says Chris. "He doesn't get anything straight."

I say, "He looks real serious."

"He says, 'Forgive us our trash baskets as we forgive those who trash-bash against us,'" Chris says.

"—Well."

"Well, that's crazy, you know it's crazy," says Chris. "He just missed the point."

"No kidding," says Chris. "Hi, Kearney."

"Hi," says Kearney in reflex. Then he sees Chris crouching in the car and says "Agggrh-hh-r" and sticks out a tongue long as a Santa Claus hat and blows a razz-berry at the car. Chris leaps to the window. "Back at you, *back*atcha, back*atcha!*"

"What's the matter?" I turn a corner, clearing the school zone and picking up speed.

"He got whipped today, he drank Miz Miley's water-colors, the green and the aqua. He dropped 'em in the flower vase and shook them around and drank them." Chris laughs. "And when we had to take off our shoes to weigh he had a hole in both toes, his feet stink."

"How about your toes?" I ask.

"One hole," says Chris. "Hi, Marvin, hey there Marvin —*hey!*"

The Green
Suitcase

THE THINGS I LIKE BEST ABOUT NEW YORK ARE THE
landings and the takeoffs. These are rich experiences indeed. The air roars in the cool corridor of the silver plane
and everyone tries to look brave for the stewardesses,
who are beautiful and friendly and somehow more *potential* than most other women. Even when they simply sit
down it is more potential and when they walk it is almost
unsettlingly potential and I don't plan to go into it any
further. At night as you slant into La Guardia you see
gardens of fuzzy blue lights, these the precise shade of

the Army's World War II athlete's-foot medicine. And beyond these, the tireless city, radiant on its bed of living rock.

I love the coming and going, it's the in-between that throws me. The time I'm actually *in* New York.

Even my suitcase is uncomfortable in New York.

Recently, before taking wing for the city, I purchased a green suitcase. In my home town it looked smart and the clerk who sold it to me said it was so durable you could lay it on the ground and jump up and down on it. He said the color went all the way through the material and would never wear off.

I discovered when I claimed the suitcase at La Guardia that it was an awful shade of green and that, in fact, any kind of green was not to be cherished in a man's luggage. The place where you claimed bags was littered with glowing brown ones of calfskin, creamy pigskin nicely saddle-stitched, coal-black cordovans.

At the hotel I anchored the suitcase near the center of the lobby and it floated there on the placid marble, serenely hideous. The desk clerk studied my drip-dry seersucker suit and gazed beyond me at the suitcase. Be it to his everlasting credit, he did not smile. I told him who I was and said I had a reservation. "I'm from Mississippi," I added foolishly. Sustained contact with New York hotel clerks always bruises and shrinks me. As I stood there in the grip of the shrinkage I had the feeling he expected me to keep talking. "Hattiesburg, Mississippi," I said.

Even when I have wired ahead for a room I have the feeling that a New York hotel is a kind of private club and that the people sitting around the lobby were subjected to stern and tricky tests before the clerk accepted them.

"We have no record of your reservation," the clerk said.

"Well, I sure wired you. Maybe you don't believe it, but I'm telling the truth."

"I'm telling the truth, too," he said. "There's no record." I feared that everyone in the lobby, all the men and women who were bona fide members of the hotel, would hear him. I hunched the shoulders of my weird seersucker, the likes of which was to be seen nowhere else in the lobby, probably nowhere along the entire Atlantic seaboard. All visible suits were dark and narrow, none wide and pale.

"Of course it doesn't matter," the clerk said. "This time of year there's no need for a reservation."

"I'd like something air-conditioned," I said weakly.

His brows lifted. Of course. *All* the rooms here were air-conditioned. And the way I'd put it to him was crude and comical; it sounded as though perhaps I wanted my car or the seat of my pants air-conditioned, nothing specific, just *something*.

Anyway, the clerk finally pledged me and a bellhop popped from the depths of the shining stone floor and rush week began. Then another bellhop appeared and one of them grabbed the suitcase. The leftover bellhop ran off somewhere the way leftover bellhops do, looking very important even though he must have had nowhere special to go. This is a noticeable thing about people in New York. Next to the fact that New York women's buttocks somehow seem more buttocky, the principal

impression is that almost everyone is hurrying to an important appointment; even the people sitting and drinking in bars strike me as drinking rather more importantly than people in other places.

In the room I tipped the bellboy and for a moment he stood there looking at the coin as if he didn't know what it was. He registered neither disappointment nor disgust. He wagged his head a fraction of an inch, glanced at my suitcase and departed. The entire scene was inconclusive and diminishing.

During my three-day stay in the city I lunched with three magazine editors, quiet kindly men. I learned shortly that I could not drink Martinis as swiftly as they did without getting drunk, but I held the pace anyway and later could remember very little of what they'd said, and yet the main reason I'd flown to New York was to hear what they had to say in regard to future work and assignments. I do remember that when we came out of this Italian restaurant after swallowing countless Martinis and some slippery veal that appeared to have been rouged and oiled, we saw a Jaguar Mark VII sedan sliding down the street and one of the editors remarked: "That leather, all that beautiful leather." And I, my head rolling loosely from side to side, said, "You mean the seats?" And the editor laughed and said, no, not just the seats, the entire car, that every inch of it was fine old British leather, even the transmission, and that a leather transmission was the quietest in the whole world, didn't I know that? Everyone laughed and looked at me and I felt that they knew about my green suitcase and what a hopeless hick I was and always would be. I remember that at some time or other one of them used the word "behest" and no one seemed to think it comical, although I was under the impression that King Arthur was the last fellow on record to employ such a word. And one of them said I must begin writing "fatter." I am certain that in the course of the luncheon many valuable and intelligent things were said, but nothing significant was able to hang on against the great cold surge of gin and general excitement.

The next day I lunched with a book-publishing editor who had written me some time ago, saying that when we met, if conversation languished, we could just eat. Conversation did that little thing and we ate in ponderous silence. Now and then he told a joke, but I lost track of the narrative during the longest of the jokes and when he gestured suddenly, pointing a finger (this was part of the joke) I thought he saw something outside the window and I twisted around in my chair and stuck an elbow in the tartar sauce. He studied me with peculiar keenness after this and seemed relieved when finally we parted.

I visited two old newspaper friends and had the feeling they found me embarrassing. Maybe it was the seersucker. Both of them had become very poised and low-key, not at all the way they were when I knew them in Denver. Sometimes they got so poised you could barely hear them and I would hear suddenly the blare of my own big, countrified mouth. The friend I used to like the most had developed a taste for eels and folk music. I ate the tip of one eel with him, to prove I could be as civilized and sick at my stomach as the next fellow and during this session it came to light he had somehow learned to read the menu in a Japanese restaurant. Nothing showy, mind you; he simply ordered his eel in that poised way and the waitress knew exactly what he was talking about.

I always figure I'm going to have the hell of a time in New York, but the pattern does not vary, and after I'm there I simply shrink and shrink and the city becomes larger and larger and puzzlinger and puzzlinger. So many of the people have the sleek, self-licked look of large Siamese cats, all of a nimble, graceful piece. I get to where I hate to go outside my hotel room. Even for a drink of cold water at the fountain downstairs. You rarely ever have enough cold water in a New York hotel. All hotel ice melts at a furious rate, but New York hotel ice is the worst; you can hear it creaking and clashing in the plastic bucket as it melts on the dresser. I believe they put something in their ice so that you will have to order more and they can gouge you for another tip.

After seeing my friend that could order an eel in Japanese I spent considerable time in my room sprawled on the stiff bed in the corner, watching TV. You hear a lot about the high grade of entertainment in New York and it is true. There was this girl on TV, a tap dancer, who had long jellylike thighs that shivered when she kicked out her foot, yet her calves seemed hard as base-balls and did not shake at all. As if that wasn't enough to hold the attention of even the most critical visitor, she could scramble round on all fours with the speed of a spider.

She was a kind of highlight of the trip. She had no great fund of poise and probably would gag on an eel, but you could understand every word she spoke or sang;

and not once during her performance did she so much as glance at the green suitcase which rested with enormous open jaws on the luggage rack at the foot of the bed.

It's Not
the Height,
It's the Hole

YOU READ ABOUT THE HEIGHT OF THE EMPIRE STATE
Building, but that's not what gave me the shivers. After
the elevator took off I was aware only of whispering
darkness beneath the cage.

I asked the elevator operator how long it would take
the cage to fall a hundred and two (or is it three?)
stories. A woman passenger shrieked faintly. She was
middle-aged and plump and dressed like Robin Hood. I
don't know if the idea of falling caused her to cry out or
if she happened to back into an umbrella.

The elevator man ignored the question. He had a nar-

row face and black eyes. There was something proud in the way he stood with his nose against the wall and in the flex of his hand at the controls. After all, here was a man who equaled the world altitude record for elevators every time he made a trip. He belonged to the company of Glenn and Schirra, Carpenter and Shepherd, an eaglet among eagles. His long nose was quite steady, it never rubbed the painted wall of the inside of the cage.

There were five of us besides the operator. The woman who had shrieked was the only female. She was dressed all in green, even green shoes and jewelry to match her suit. From the crown of her green hat two long skinny green feathers projected droopingly. You had the feeling that if you boosted her into a tree she would eat leaves. There were two Japanese in gray suits with identical dark blue umbrellas. And there was a seaman of the United States Navy, his white pants so tight they seemed to lift him now and again to the balls of his feet. You had the uneasy feeling the crotch of the pants might at any instant explode, causing great damage if not death in this confined space.

I asked again the question about the cage falling.

"We got safety devices," the operator said finally, hitching up his britches, using the insides of his wrists in the Cagney manner.

"What if the devices *fail?*" My own questions were frightening me and I wished I would shut up.

"They can't," he said contemptuously. "They were designed by engineers. You know, college fellas."

"I don't care who designed this crate," said the seaman, riding on the balls of his feet. "She could take a tumble."

The Japanese nodded calmly and the green woman whuffed out her cheeks and closed her eyes.

"It's all automatic," the operator said. "Anything gets wrong with it, the safety stuff flips into gear, you know what I mean?"

"Naw," said the seaman, teetering.

The Japanese shook their heads and smiled identical smiles. The green woman now had the look of someone who has received notice of a shockingly large overdraft. She tried to smile, but the thin fluorescent mouth was slack.

You heard the strumming of cables in the shaft and in that instant we swayed to a halt high above the ceaseless city. I wished I'd gone shopping with Mary even though she is a poor shopper and had told me that the day before she could not even find the basement at Gimbel's and that many people in the store did not seem to know there was a place dug out under it with cheaper prices than upstairs. How differently these elevator cables strummed than the short fat greasy ones of the three-story newspaper building back home. These cables sounded thin and hysterical, almost vicious, power-mad and conscienceless. You felt they would as soon snap as strum.

There was a mild ringing in the top of the skull. "You transfer here," said the operator to the wall. The door hissed open. He seemed glad to be rid of us as we streamed out into the gray light of floor seventy-something. I started to tell him that I myself had spent four and a half years in college and couldn't string wire for a clothesline, but it seemed a cruel thing to do.

§ 174 §

You imagined him as an old man, jockeying a freight elevator in some miserable ten-story building, boring his associates to tears with tales of the greatest hole in the world. On the skids, without a shred of guts or confidence left to him, a grounded and crippled falcon feeding on memories.

Now he was gone. The sliding door chuffed shut as abruptly as the blade of a cigar cutter. We took another elevator to the top, feeling more secure, but wondering if the hole beneath this new elevator went all the way to the ground, or if it was plugged off at the level where we boarded it.

I asked the new operator. He shrugged as if it made no difference to him one way or the other.

As for the top of the Empire State Building, all I can say is that on a rainy day you do not see a great deal, what with the water whipping around in sheets and steaming off warm stone. It's not the way you think it is up there. You'd imagined it would be thrillingly easy to fall off, but they've got iron fences and a great deal of glass, too. Initials of honeymooning women and other excited people with diamonds have been cut in the glass.

Up top it's really dull as mutton and you understand why so many veteran New Yorkers don't have the slightest idea what's in, or on, the Empire State Building.

But if you ever get a chance you owe it to yourself to take a ride in that big hole. That's the hair-raising wonder of the thing.

Sex
and the Writer

I SAW A SEXUAL-ATTRACTION RATING LIST THE OTHER day in the paper and writers were ranked only a hair under doctors and quite a bit ahead of astronauts. That same night I saw a TV movie in which a beautiful young girl suffered the shimmying shudders every time an aged writer laid a hand on her or said something pretty. She was not shuddering from revulsion, but because she was burning right down to the tips of her little painted toes.

The whole thing is getting funnier and funnier, because who makes up the sex-appeal lists and who writes the scripts for such movies?

Writers.

Now you can't blame writers for wanting the world to think of them as sex lions, but it is time the truth was told because if it isn't, a lot of girls who could snag themselves a lawyer or a pipe fitter (more later about pipe fitters) will be setting their caps for writers. There are not enough writers to go around and even if there were it would be a rotten deal for the girls.

Every girl should be instructed at an early age that when a writer has a spare moment he just likes to lie down alone with his hands over his eyes, and that often his breath is bad from too many cigarettes and cheese sandwiches.

A writer has poor muscle tone from long hours of sitting in a chair and this does not make for stamina or sustained excitement, even if a girl is able to get him to rouse himself and remove his hands from his eyes. He is rattled by small situations and may spend an entire morning reading what he wrote the night before and cursing. Usually he has a right to curse because it is pretty bad, if not downright humiliating. When he isn't reading or cursing or writing or lying down he hangs around the mailbox waiting for the news that he has become rich and famous, and this in time becomes quite a strain on the nerves because the odds against fame and wealth shouldn't happen even to a daily-doubles player. The writer knows this. So he smokes even more cigarettes and eats more cheese sandwiches. He drinks up the money he has saved to send his manuscripts out by registered mail. Incidentally, he is forever licking the flaps of Manila envelopes and this, while not habit-forming, does nothing for the breath. The breath of a writer would kill a young Douglas fir.

In this TV movie I saw, Greer Garson is married to Douglas Fairbanks, Jr., a writer who wants to go chasing off to some scented isle in Greece with a beautiful younger girl. The girl has already driven up to Maine and back with him on a kind of shakedown cruise and now she wants to go to Greece too. Greer knows all about it. She says fine, but that the girl had better look out, that Doug is just using the affair to "regenerate" his talent, like he always does between books. That's how Doug charges up his writing battery. Direct current. Then, so long, kid. Practically in cold blood, Greer says, fondling all seventeen of Doug, Jr.'s, fat novels which are leather bound and arranged in order of date of publication, on a shelf. Greer says the books are her "children," that they are all she cares anything about.

I tried to imagine my wife Mary down on her knees in the kitchen pantry caressing the cardboard box that contains my lifework. Mary stores my published stuff there when she stores it at all. It lies under a bale of recipes for shrimp Creole, hot-tamale pie and several hangover remedies conceived and practiced by her late Uncle Joe. On top of all of it is an oddly blurred arc of blue plastic, the remains of a hula hoop Jecca placed on the barbecue grill when she was younger and more imaginative.

Recently a publishing firm wished to reissue an arty little novel of mine about a $100-a-night call girl and a murderer who teamed up to knock off an armored car. It developed we did not have a copy in the house to send to the publisher who needed a spare; and if my mother had not hung onto a copy I expect there would have been no reprint at all.

Probably the only reason my mother kept it was because in a moment of whimsy I had dedicated it to my grandmother, who was a devout Baptist and a leader of the Lottie Moon Circle. The dedication puzzled my mother and when things were dull she would open the front of the book and stare at it for minutes on end, trying to reconcile what was inside the book with what was inside my grandmother, my mother's mother.

Now, about pipe fitters. The greatest real-life lover I ever knew was in my World War II platoon in the Philippines; I mean he *must* have been, because he'd been married fifteen years and his wife, who was a waitress, tried to stow herself away on a boat at San Francisco and come to him, to this pipe fitter whom we shall call Walmsley. She mailed him pieces of Kleenex that she had kissed and once she mailed him her diaphragm to prove she didn't need it till he returned. He showed it all around at a small beer party we had in our tent near Tacloban and some of the fellows were moved to tears, not by the diaphragm itself, but by the unabashed sentiment behind it.

I lost track of Walmsley later in Japan, but on board the troopship headed for North Honshu he still had in his possession that remarkable testimonial. Several times in crap games in the hold of the ship he was cleaned of cash and someone offered to roll him for it, but Walmsley said no, that some things were more important than money. He said it wasn't just any old diaphragm, that it belonged to Sarah and had been fitted for their honeymoon by a doctor who was a graduate of Tulane University, one of the finest medical schools of the south, if not the nation.

Here was a truly sensitive and worthy lover, a man who had to have absolute quiet in order to write his own name.

Don't speak to me of the lovableness of *writers*.

Visit
to a Two-Finger
Typist

IN THE SUMMER OF 1961, A YEAR BEFORE THE DEATH of William Faulkner, I decided on a rather nutty pilgrimage to Charlottesville on the chance of interviewing him. Also, I had the idea that some of his profundity and resounding thoughtfulness might rub off onto me. Mary seemed to think it a dashing if not a logical plan, in view of the fact that Faulkner was notoriously uncommunicative and would not even talk to a stranger on the telephone. Jecca, who even then was bucking for ballet instruction, said she bet Faulkner's daughters all studied or *had* studied toe dancing, and I said yes, all twenty-two of them had, and they grew their own lambs just to clip the lamb's wool and pack it around their toes when they danced; and that they danced only in the moonlight on the roofs of crumbling Southern colonial mansions. Jecca said, not really disrespectfully, that she bet her toes could be trained for two or three months on what it would cost to travel to Virginia to see a man who didn't want to see me.

For a long time I'd hoped to write a story about my fellow Mississippian. I wanted to do a plain and unpretentious little piece on Faulkner the Man. I'd read a number of magazine yarns about the sixty-three-year-old Nobel Prize winner, and in each of these the interviewer sounded awestruck, almost frightened, and full of literary soul searching. My account would be light and rather humorous. After all, here was a man who, despite his stature as a writer, must bicker with his children, get his thumb caught in the sink, cope with an aging gall bladder. Or so I had thought before actually laying eyes on him.

I tried half a dozen times to arrange an interview while Faulkner was at his home in Oxford, but one of his daughters told me he wouldn't come to the phone and he declined to answer my letters, in which I made the sentences as long and beautiful and confusing as was possible within the framework of my scant talents, knowing that he admired and elected to manufacture eerie overweight sentences in his own work. In the summer and fall, however, he was a resident writer at the University of Virginia in Charlottesville and that is where I finally found him.

I caught up first with another of his daughters, who

also lives in Charlottesville. She directed me to her father's home, but said, "I can't guarantee you success. I can only tell you where to find him and you'll just have to take your chances. It will depend on his mood, whether he liked his breakfast—you know." She was a slender blonde with a nice figure and I did not realize until later I'd forgotten to ask her if she ever danced on her toes.

I followed directions and arrived at a two-story brick Georgian house. There was a dusty little red Rambler station-wagon with a Mississippi tag parked in the drive-way. The front door of the house was open and I could hear the clack of a typewriter, a steady two-fingered whacking. It occurred to me as I pressed the bell that I hadn't expected William Faulkner's typewriter to sound so commonplace. In fact, I'd never thought of it making any kind of noise at all. It seemed shocking that any manual labor, no matter how mild, should be involved in his transfer of thought to paper.

I thumbed the button again, sweat tickling my cheeks as the typing faltered, then ceased. He materialized quietly in the doorway, absolutely composed and motion-less as a photograph. I had the feeling I was staring at a picture on the dust jacket of one of his books.

"I'm sorry," I said. "I'm sorry to interrupt you this way."

He inclined the fine gray, almost white, head as if he agreed that I should be sorry. He spoke in a soft, patient voice, the words barely moving the gray moustache: "Whom did you wish to see, sir?"

"Ah, you sir," I said foolishly, feeling flustered. "I drove a thousand miles to see you."

This seemed to make him almost sick at his stomach. He winced. Just a flicker of a wince. I explained that I was from Hattiesburg, a fellow Mississippian, and that I'd tried to telephone him but had been told he wouldn't answer the phone.

"That's right, sir." He stood now unblinking in the doorway. "What is it you want from me?"

I tried to explain, but the sun was beating down on my head and I was tired and my eyes burned from the long trip and I'm afraid I jabbered. I said that I'd always admired him and suspected that some of his short stories were the best ever written, and that one of them, a piece about a little boy who followed his big brother to an army induction center, was the most moving thing I had ever read. I said that another one, which was mostly an account of two women chasing a mule out of a yard, was more exciting to me than Hemingway's bridge-dynamiting stuff and how could a writer do so much with just a mule and two women?

He sighed, studying me thoughtfully. "You come on in and we'll see what we can do to help you."

In the living room he sighed again and sat on a couch. He began stuffing his pipe, very slowly. He motioned me to a chair. "I have no patience with a certain kind of interview," he said. "The kind where a man comes to me and asks me to say something that will interest his readers. That kind of thing is grotesque, you must realize that."

As I sat opposite him I understood why so many writers had failed. You interview Faulkner on his own terms if at all; and you would no more ask him about his gall bladder than you would pinch the tip of his elegant nose. He was a tiny man of enormous dignity. He radiated a kind of quiet strength. The feeling of quiet was the primary impression; it was in the voice, the movement of the hands, the way he walked, the controlled glitter of his almost black and hooded eyes.

"So," he said, sipping at the stem of his pipe. "Just what, specifically, do you want?"

I very rarely know specifically what I want of others or even of myself. This, if there is a story, is the story of my life. When I go to a drive-in I'm not even certain if I want onions on my hamburger. I cackled uncertainly, abandoning once and for all the brash business of sink and gall bladder. "I just want to write about the way you work," I said, making it up as I went along. "You know, your working schedule, the tools. . . ."

He uncrossed his legs and sat up straighter on the couch, growing and growing. "Why no, no sir," he said. "I wouldn't tolerate that at all, I figure it's nobody's business but my own. You mean, sir, you wish to follow me around and write down everything I do?"

"Oh, no," I cried out in anguish. "Not that, not that at all." Watching him grow, seeing how he sprouted from that couch, I felt hopelessly impaled on the moment, like a bug beneath glass. Here was a man who could have said to a daughter: "No, no ma'am, there will be no toe-dancing lessons until we can afford them," and that would have been *that.*

"I could not tolerate that," he repeated calmly.

I waggled my head, which felt large and unrefined. "Of course not."

I asked him about his job as resident writer. What did it mean to be a resident writer?

§ *186* §

"There ain't much to it," he said. "There really ain't much to it. You just live here some of the time and you walk around and people see you and say, well, there he is, there he goes. I don't have any kind of an office at the university and I give no lectures. Once in a while I meet with a group and answer questions about writing. If a man has a problem, some *specific* question about writing, I will try to help him. But like I say, I will not talk just to be talking."

He said the idea of living part of the time there in the rolling foothills of Virginia appealed to him because he loved horses and dogs and liked fox hunting. Every morning around six o'clock he arose and drove to his stables on the edge of town, riding for an hour or more before returning to the house for a shower, breakfast and work. "There is something about jumping a horse over a fence, something that makes you feel good. Perhaps it's the risk, the gamble. In any event it's a thing I need."

He said he set himself no regular work schedule at the typewriter. "If you feel you have to write ten pages a day it takes the fun out of it, and the work suffers. Writing is hard work but it should be fun, it always has been to me. I've never felt any other way about it. I'm an amateur writer, I'm not a literary man."

What, then, was a literary man?

Faulkner considered that a literary man was some-one preoccupied with the idea of writing for "the benefit of literature—a thing I've not done."

This of course was subject to argument but you didn't argue it with Faulkner in his own living room. It was plainly no pose with him. He believed a literary man had to select carefully everything he wrote or said. Faulkner said people knew how he himself felt in this regard and every time he opened his mouth they didn't expect him to come out with something magnificent. He could say, for instance, "Pass the potatoes," and no one was unduly disappointed.

"Your writing life and your regular life are separate things and should remain separate," Faulkner said. "Because writing is a thing born of the imagination and confined largely to the imagination. Of course a writer is going to write, that goes without saying, and the only thing he can do when the demon's on his back is to write it off.

"In the beginning, before a writer has made his stake, he must have another job to sustain him, or he must be a tramp who doesn't give a damn how he lives.

"I don't believe there's anything to this idea that a writer does better if he can go off in the woods somewhere and hole up away from the world. I think that if his stuff is any good it will be good in a hole in the woods, but it would have been just as good anywhere else. And if it's bad it will be as bad in a hole in the woods."

What about the writer who claims he can't sell anything because his product is too uncommon to appeal to the masses?

"I've known quite a few writers and never have seen one whose stories were too *good* to be published. This, of course, is a very comfortable attitude and no doubt serves its purpose. But you may be certain with all the bad stuff being published these days, the really good things are bound to sell. It is inevitable. You can't fail with truly good writing, it will surely reach the public. There's nothing to the mute, inglorious Milton business."

§ *188* §

As Faulkner spoke in low tones, the voice almost inaudible at times, a few decibles above a whisper, but not weak, only quiet, he paused occasionally to peer into the glowing bowl of his pipe. The pipe seemed a part of his hand. "Financial success is not likely to hurt a writer who is a writer, because, you see, he never produces the perfect story of his dreams. He may satisfy other people but not himself. And every morning he has something to wake up to, every morning of his life, another chance to try for that perfect story. A carpenter may build the flawless house and a bricklayer may raise the perfect wall, but with a writer it never happens and he must keep on with it."

I told him many citizens of my town claimed to know him and that a remarkable number professed genuine palship with him. They even recalled exchanging profound truths with him while attending Ole Miss back in the days when he fired boilers and studied there.

Faulkner smiled, the mustache not smiling with him because it is a full one, too full to join in a smile. "I don't believe the good people of Mississippi ever will understand how a man can sit in the shade and make $30,000 for defacing a few scraps of paper (the Nobel Prize paid that amount). In Mississippi the people work for their money and you can understand how they feel about writing, why it puzzles them. In Mississippi a man goes out in the sun and sweats for his dollars."

Was he working on another novel?

"I always say no in answer to that question, I never say yes."

"But are you?"

"No."

"I heard you typing a while ago, it sounded like two fingers."

"It was, it always is."

"Index fingers?"

"Yes."

I felt a radiant warmth stealing into my own typing fingers. I am an index-finger man myself and now, for the first time, was not ashamed of it. "Would you mind if I took a look at your typewriter? You know, just looked at it so I can say I've seen the machine you use?"

"No use to look, it's my youngest daughter's. I don't like to lug my old portable back and forth between Charlottesville and Oxford. She lets me use hers when I'm here." He said his typewriter at Oxford probably was one of the oldest in the country, about forty years of age and still in good working order. "I don't need anything fancy for these two fingers, it will last as long as I need it, I guess."

And it did.

Tom Wolfe's
Brother
Still Goes
Wah-Wah-Wah

IT IS 9:15 P.M., OCTOBER 3, 1962, AND I AM STANDING IN the middle of Spruce Street in Asheville, N. C., in front of "Dixieland," the old boardinghouse immortalized in Thomas Wolfe's resounding, rebounding novel *Look Homeward, Angel;* and I am shaking hands with Luke Gant, who stammers and waves his arms and laughs *wah-wah-wah* just as he did in the book. There is a light shining upstairs in the bay-windowed bedroom where Ben Gant died and another glows through blue-and-peach stained glass of a downstairs window, the room where old man Gant expired after an heroic bout with a cancerous prostate and various members of his clan.

"W-www-wuh-well, it's nice to meet you," says Luke, who in real life is Fred Wolfe. He flails long tweed arms and smiles and says in answer to a question: "Yes, I'm g-gguilty of every damn thing Tom accused me of in the book, and more besides. M-mmm-my opinion, Tom took it pretty easy on me, he said I was an *upright* young man."

He slashes the air with a large hand and again flashes the good smile. His hair is almost white but there is plenty of it. Pink plastic spectacle frames glisten in reflected light. Luke, or rather Fred, is sixty-eight now. But it is not difficult to understand why his late and brilliant brother admired him both in and out of print. Even the stammering, described faithfully in the book, sounds good coming from Luke's wide, energetic mouth. I must call him Luke, because ever since I read *Look Homeward, Angel* I've wanted to meet Luke.

Parks Department workmen are stacking with a clatter a couple of hundred wooden chairs in the street in front of the house, cleaning up in the wake of the annual Thomas Wolfe birthday party. "D-did you enjoy the show?" asks Luke.

"Yes, it was fine. I liked it fine."

He appears pleased. A friend of his, a doctor, bears down on him, shakes his hand and calls out to the dispersing crowd, "Hey, everybody, here's Luke, this is old Luke if you want to talk to him." At the moment there are not takers and the doctor exits, looking crestfallen. Luke looks after him a moment, rubs a square jaw, and says: "The old house is just about the way it used to b-be. Almost everything. It makes me feel kind of funny. I'm the only one left, you know. Momma and Poppa, Ben and Tom and Mabel, all the others are gone, and when I come to one of these things it makes me feel kind of funny."

It is worse than kind of funny. It is kind of spooky. Because Luke, if anything, is even Lukier than in the book, and as we stand there breathing the same misty altitudinous air they breathed in the book, in the shadows of the same giant maples, I can almost hear the boarders of long ago grumbling and giggling on the broad porch of the house; can almost discern the panting whisperings of Eugene Gant and the older woman who overheated him with moonlit kisses and left him squirming and lonely.

Did Luke really roar down that hill in the car, as Tom had chronicled?

"Ye-yess, it was a 1913 Ford, it wasn't Momma's new Reo, the one she bought and kept in the carriage house and wouldn't let anyone drive. It was a model-T and on a steep hill it would go like a bat out of hell. It's a wonder I didn't k-k-kill us all."

And did Luke really have a *wah-wah-wah* laughing fit in the funeral home and did he wear a Roman soldier costume on the stage in Atlanta? "Yes, like I say it was all t-t-true about me, except I don't know how *up*right I was in those days. In a manner of speaking I *was* upright, but it wouldn't do to describe wah-wah-wah."

After a time Luke says he must leave. "My brother-in-law Ralph Wheaton is flat on his back—I'm staying with him a few days. He's eighty-one now. My God, how the years wheel by! He was married to my sister Mabel, she was Helen in the book, had a real big part in the book if you remember. Ralph was the cash-register salesman in the book. I hate to see him down on his back this way, but he's wearing out, you know, we all wear out, don't we?"

I say yes, we all wear out.

"Goodbye now," says Luke. "If you ever get over to Spartanburg, look me up. I'm retired and don't have much to do. I used to work for Foremost Dairies." He is still smiling as he walks away and several people stop him a dozen paces from me. He grins for them and throws his arms around in the set pattern, like an exhausted but still vigorous actor who has played a role so many times the movements and responses are programed beyond alteration. In a way he is entrapped, for he must continue, at the age of sixty-eight, to play himself the way he was in his twenties, and it is not an easy thing to snort smoke when the fire is dying in the furnace. He is Luke. It is more than a role, it is a responsibility. He is good-natured, high-octane, outgoing and unpretentious Luke, the final shred of life remaining of the principal characters of The Novel. People come from miles around to see him and lay hands on him and to say to each other that Luke is still a *caution*, the spit image of his old self. Why, it's a dogfooted miracle the way Tom got it all down on paper as clear as day.

Luke says now to his new audience: "Yes, I finally got an electrical engineering degree from Georgia Tech. But it took me ten years, too long to get that part of it in the book, what with flunking out and working and going back; and then when I got the degree I didn't engineer.

Wah-wah-wah-wah. I remember the last time I went back to Georgia Tech, the fourth time, the registrar said, 'My God, not you again!' "

He sounds very tired when finally he gets away.

Forty or fifty of the more than two hundred persons who came to the birthday observance are still in the street, talking in front of the white-painted, two-storied frame house, which is maintained now by the city as a literary shrine. The place that Tom Wolfe despised has become a mecca for his admirers. It is probably the last place or thing in the world he would wish to be associated with him. There is some very fancy conversation in the street. A large gray lady says to her companion, a camel-hairish, towering man with a dramatically pukka Indian-Service-type moustache: "When I stand here I can just hear old Gant roaring, I can see him building those huge fires against the cold and the darkness. Those fires. I can't forget them. Surely they were symbolic."

"Of course," her companion yawns, sounding as if it had never occurred to him that Gant would build other than symbolic fires.

"I was a schoolgirl in Akron when I read *Angel* and it gave me the shivers. I read it over and over. I fell in love with Ben, he was so white-faced and brave and he worked all night, coughing his head off, but not feeling sorry for himself."

"Of course," the man says, absently pinching his pukka moustache.

A small man in a creamy Sinatra-looking raincoat tells a smaller woman in an identical and smaller coat: "Wolfe was strictly a sensualist, he wrote of his sensations, he couldn't write action worth a damn." The man does not say so, but he implies that there is something dishonest, perhaps even unforgivable in the business of writing of one's sensations at the expense of action.

The woman says she is glad the show tonight was taken from what she considered the finest of the four novels, *Look Homeward, Angel*. She gets across the message that she has read all four and without making it explicit expresses her doubts that the man in the matching raincoat even *knew* there were four.

The show had been a matter of tape recordings and lights, readings from the book amplified by loudspeakers spotted around the house. No visible actors, just voices which seemed to boom from the various rooms, mood music and a few sound effects, the best of the latter being Ben's coughing. A spate of beautiful words and spotlights squirting strawberry and frosty blue against the house. There was Ben's death scene upstairs, the light popping on inside the room for this; and when Helen was married the light flared in the parlor and so on. "It was beautiful, starkly beautiful," says the little woman in the creamy coat. I thought personally that there was too much done with the lights and that at times the old place looked as if it were burning down in the middle of a scene which called for serenity. At one point a workman ran out into the yard to adjust a baby spot and he stumbled and his spread-eagled shadow fell on the house, momentarily swallowing it, so that the voices, cavernous and tortured, emerged from the stomach of the shadow.

As one old-timer says to me, and I agree: "If Tom could of been here tonight he would of laughed his ass off."

I move around in the crowd, reluctant to leave, and I

meet a Mrs. Ina Isbell, a neat woman of medium size, who says she is hostess in the house, that she is employed by the city of Asheville to guide people through the place and answer questions. People ask her some funny ones. One fellow wanted to know if old W. O. Gant might have outlived Eugene, his son (Thomas Wolfe) if back in those days surgeons had been able to whisk out a diseased prostate the way they do nowadays. He said that now such an operation caused barely a furrow in the brow of Blue Cross.

Mrs. Isbell says she told him she really couldn't say. She indicates that she knows very little of prostates.

She says this is the second year of the show and it was supposed to be the preceding night but was rained out; that this is the first time she has seen the show from the outside. Last year she was inside the house, running up and down stairs, popping on lights and turning them off, a list of cues in one hand and a tiny pencil torch in the other: "I held the light close to the floor so it wouldn't show outside. If you could see the light climbing the stairs it wouldn't be at all realistic. I ran those stairs till my tongue hung out."

Now they have a central control panel in the house and you simply press buttons to handle the interior lights.

We go into the house and Mrs. Isbell shows me around. There are several visitors in the entrance hall and they are talking about writers and writing in the juicy tones some people reserve for these things. A man is saying: "I understand New York was the only place he could write well; that seems damned strange, doesn't it? They say once he holed up in a cabin here on the mountain, but for some reason it made him want to stay drunk and he couldn't find his typewriter with both hands. . . ."

There is a picture of Tom, aged six, on the wall of the hall, dark curls falling to his collar, the rims of the nails of his clasped hands appearing suspiciously dark.

A couple stands before the picture. They are talking in low tones, rapidly. It seems they own or operate a sporting goods store either in Asheville or in some out-lying town and what they are discussing, thank heaven, has nothing to do with literature. One of their employees is a woman who, as I understand from the conversation, is no longer young. And this no-longer-young woman's regular job is to sew numerals on athletic jerseys. This in itself is fascinating if not compelling news because no one ever even wonders about how the numbers get onto the jerseys. Anyway, what this number-sewer likes to do is come out on the floor of the store and sell football shoes. "I *told* her selling football shoes is a man's job and to *leave* it to the men," the man sighs. "I don't understand it at all, she keeps dropping what she is doing and Lord knows we need her at the sewing machine, but out she sails and before anyone knows what she's up to, there she is again, selling football shoes."

We go upstairs and I look at the bed in which all the Wolfe children were born. Mrs. Wolfe's bed is enormous. A mare could have been delivered of a colt in it. Some of Tom's clothing was in a glass case. Ben's deathbed is made of iron, quite depressing.

On the way out Mrs. Isbell shows me Luke's engineering degree on a wall of the room she uses downstairs as an office. She says she doesn't know why Luke never engineered; but that he really built a name for himself as a salesman for Foremost Dairies at Spartanburg. "He comes back here every ten days or so, just to walk around and look at things and talk. He charges around and jokes and laughs, but, you know, sometimes I think he is a little lonely."

Von Braun
Has
No Gold
Feathers

COCOA BEACH, FLA.—A SERGEANT OF THE AIR FORCE
whose thumb was swaddled and splinted told me he'd
smashed it three times this spring while he was trying to
get a Titan ready for a shoot. He said two of his buddies,
both corporals, had ruined perfectly good index fingers
as the result of slipped wrenches while they were mon-
keying with the Titan.

This is an aspect of the space age that very few people
consider. I had not planned to consider it myself, but the
sergeant practically insisted when he learned this was

my first visit to Canaveral, a flat sandy area where most of the buildings are correspondingly flat and so are the haircuts of the sunburned men who crush their fingers in the interests of science. Space shooting is old hat here. People don't even put down their drinks and walk outside when a rocket leaves the pad to whirl around the world.

The sergeant said, after ordering another whiskey sour, that all of the gee-whiz had gone out of it and that Jane Mansfield could be shot bareback to the moon and the old regulars wouldn't even turn around to look.

He said everyone on the "outside" was in awe of the Cape and the missile program and it was enough to make a cow laugh to hear greenhorns talk about Wernher von Braun, as if the German scientist had gold tail feathers and swallowed liquid oxygen and kerosene every morning for breakfast. "Mind you, Mister von Braun is as fine as they come. I have seen him in person and he smiles at you like his wife wouldn't mind borrowing a cup of cornmeal if they needed it. But all this space-worship is crazy, and he'd be the first to tell you. No matter how you cut it, a missile is just a skinful of fuel and feeder pipes."

He added: "They're just big skyrockets like the ones you used to launch from pop bottles in the backyard. So they're five stories tall. So what?"

Although the sergeant's whiskey sour did not seem to be spreading any sunshine inside him, his talk cheered me. He gave me the feeling there was no reason why an ordinary fellow like myself should not be able to grasp the missile program as well as the next man. No complicated chatter about fuel thrust or metallurgical research here. This was the greenest of the grass roots of rocketry, a man who actually mashed his thumb in the service of the Titan.

In a gush of confidence I admitted that the only science I'd studied in school was a course in geology where we sat around a table with little hammers and tapped rocks and tried to guess how old they were.

"There's not a thing wrong with that," the sergeant said comfortingly.

I flushed with pleasure.

"One of the smartest men I ever knew was crazy about rocks, used to keep them all colors in the drawer with his handkerchiefs," said the sergeant, nodding sagely.

I bought him another whiskey sour.

"All of *this*," he laughed without humor, shrugging, or rather waving, his shoulders to include the entire desolate stretch of sand and scrub. "Just try and find a rock around here."

"You could collect seashells," I offered timidly, supposing he wished something handy and rigid and colorful to place in the drawer with his own handkerchiefs.

"Snot the point, snot the point."

"Oh."

"The point," said the sergeant kindly, "is on the Outside people think this is something big here and we don't even have a single Goddamned rock."

"I'm sorry."

"Just show me a rock and I'll eat it."

We had a few more drinks and after a time he convinced me he was serious about this so I went outside looking for a rock for him to eat, but he was right—there wasn't one anywhere that I could see. The ocean sounded like a hundred miles of cellophane crinkling against the shore, crackling and hissing. There were stars the size of saucers.

I went back in and told him that I couldn't find a rock, and he became extremely sarcastic and said what in the hell kind of a friend was I, anyway? I said I didn't know, that I guess I was the kind of a friend that couldn't locate a rock when a buddy was hungry for one.

"Snot the point."

It got to where no matter how reasonable I was, or how carefully responsive to his questions and half-questions, he would find something wrong and begin snotting the point in such a loud voice the bartender became unhappy. I returned to my room and wrote a letter to Mary and tried to get started on a magazine piece but finally just fell across the bed and slept. In the middle of the night I heard a whoosh and I glanced out the window and sure enough, there she went, a big one, tail winking smaller and smaller. In two minutes I was asleep again.

In the morning I had to pile out early and tour the missile base with a large group of "outsiders."

I hoped our guiding officers would keep it all as simple as the sergeant did, and just admit, from the beginning, that there wasn't much to it.

Electronic
Blackjack

I DON'T THINK THESE BRIGHT YOUNG PEOPLE WHO develop machines like electronic brains quite know what they're doing. I played cards with a brain the other day, and I came away with the distinct feeling that a take-over of men by their machines is a real possibility.

But what first struck me was that the electronic brain didn't seem at all snobbish.

It settled down to a game of blackjack like a regular fellow, ribbed you when you went bust, encouraged you to have another try. Now and again it gave out with an iron chuckle, simmered thoughtfully, cackled, and dealt another hand. It was about four feet wide and three feet tall, dressed tastefully in gray-painted metal and stainless steel, perhaps a bit square-shouldered by Ivy League standards. I had the feeling that under proper circumstances the machine would not be averse to a beer and a few saucy jokes.

Jack Munn, assistant professor of mathematics at the University of Southern Mississippi, introduced me to the brain in its air-conditioned quarters on the campus. Munn said the $87,500 machine, despite its roaring I.Q., enjoyed slumming through a session of blackjack when there was nothing more important to do.

After Munn had fed the proper taped program into the brain its electrically operated typewriter clacked out: "How much do you bet?"

Using the keys of the same typewriter I punched out my bet of $12.

"Too much," the machine answered.

Munn explained that the house stakes of this particular brain do not exceed $9.99. It has the ability to add or subtract or multiply staggering sums in a matter of milliseconds and can store 8,008 words or instructions or numbers in its transistorized memory; but when it plays blackjack it wants no part of biggety bets.

Now, as every schoolboy knows, the perfect score in blackjack is 21. Anything over that knocks you in the head. Face cards count 10 points each, the ace is either one or 11 points, depending on how it fits best in your hand. The numbered cards retain their own numerical values. But where were the playing cards? Munn, with the suavity of a Monaco croupier, quickly explained that the machine stored all 52 card symbols inside its dust-free noggin' and, barring some kind of mechanical breakdown, it wouldn't cheat for anything.

Okay by me. I decided to change my bet to $5.

"Shuffling," the brain typed, the words clattering darkly onto a roll of green and white striped paper. "Cut."

I twisted around in the chair and looked at Munn. He said the machine expected nothing further of me at the moment, that it had simply informed me what it was doing, this in a spirit of good fellowship because it realized I could not see and that perhaps I felt a bit uneasy.

It dealt me a deuce and a 6, printing the denomination of the cards on the roll of paper. It dealt itself a deuce and asked politely, "Card?"

"*Oui,*" I typed, hoping in a correspondingly good-natured way to confuse it.

It dealt me a J-D (Jack of diamonds) and I stood pat while it busted itself with a K-H (King of hearts) and a K-S (King of spades). It realized instantly it had gone bust and printed the admission that it owed me a fiver. For funsy. It did not say for funsy; all it said was, "Score $5.00." But we both knew.

I wished that my mother could see me now as I bested this lofty accumulation of electricity in a game which combined daring and mathematics. I recalled the desolate aching hours of a rainy night when my mother sought to implant the homely truth that nine times six was fifty-four. She'd sat me in a corner and placed a raincoat over my head. "Think about it," she'd said. "Think about it, son."

This feeling of warm exultation persisted as I continued for a time to outwit and outplay the brain. I wished Mary and the kids could see me. They generally beat me at such card games as Battle and Go Fish and Concentration, especially at Concentration, which is pure mechanical memory, a competition in which the dullest chimpanzee could excel providing he had the ordinary knack of recalling that the 10 of clubs had flashed fifteen minutes ago just to the left of the Jack of diamonds and three cards north of the torn place in the living-room rug.

I became quite mischievous with the machine, drawing on my thin store of foreign languages whenever the brain asked if I wanted a card. It understood perfectly the meaning of *ja, nein, si* and responded also to *nope*. Once I requested a zero card. "This is not in my vocabulary," the brain said, vibrant with humble camaraderie.

It was a good loser, as I said to Munn at the time and as I'll say now. No sulking. It took it like a sport and when, $53 ahead of the game, I pretended I was going to quit, it shuddered slightly but asked as nicely as ever, "Cards?"

"Nope."

It shuddered again and was silent, probably pondering a moonshot or the number of atoms contained in the ash of Munn's cigar. Just biding its time. After a spell I had to return to the contest, completely won over by the brain's show of humility in the face of rather raw odds. Maybe I'm nothing at Go Fish or Battle, but after all, the machine was only three or four years old and I'd been playing blackjack the better part of half a century. No matter who, or *what,* you were, it takes time to season a player, to hone him down to the perfect edge of caution and recklessness so essential in this game.

It busted me on the next deal.

"Bad show," it rattled out. "Try again."

Thinking back on it now in the sour light of resentment, I believe it was at this precise moment that the brain's real personality reared its nasty, venomous head.

During the following half-hour it busted and rebusted me. It smashed me. It wiped out my winnings and plunged me into an abyss of theoretical debt, working with a cold thoroughness that was beginning to embarrass Munn and two of his students who'd dropped in to watch the fun.

"Tough!" the brain typed, bashing me again. As it dealt the cards, the typewriter, which earlier had sounded merry and brisk, now made a noise that sounded like a culvertful of derisive crickets. "Score $103.00."

I chewed the insides of my cheeks.

The math students drifted out of the room and Munn pretended to busy himself with some test papers. At intervals he would come and stand at my shoulder but I noticed that he would not look me in the eye. He offered no comment when I observed that the machine, for all its ability to solve problems in distillation, business management and molecular structure, was rather *chicken*. It would hit itself if its hand totaled 16 points but it never would hit on 17, which is plain horse sense; nevertheless it irritated me because it would try to get me to take another card when I was sitting on a fat 20.

One time I had a 9 and a deuce. This meant a face card or a 10 would give me 21.

"*Press?*" the brain asked, practically jumping up and down on the vinyl tiles in its excitement.

To press means to bet double on a gleaming opportunity. I pressed. The brain hit me with a 3. Then it dealt me a lousy one-eyed Jack. I was unhorsed. The brain murmured and blinked several bloodshot plastic buttons. It trembled and giggled.

For the next hour it blackjacked the ears off me, dealing itself an interminable series of aces and face cards. It alternated the face cards with 10s but never seemed anywhere near running out of its fine supply of aces, stringing them out like the pickets on a fence.

As the contest progressed the atmosphere cooled and hardened. I'd started off feeling dazedly congenial, flattered that the brain would bother with me when it could be ripping into problems in thermal distribution. I had the feeling it knew, in the depths of its magnetic-drum memory, that I'd flunked freshman math in college and that once my mother had thrown that raincoat over me.

I lit a cigarette and blinked and tried to twinkle, but it didn't come off. I saw with absolute clarity the ultimate nightmare of automation, a world in which a sprinkling of these machines would convene regularly at the Bureau of Standards headquarters in Washington and play enough blackjack to clean out the entire male population of the planet. While back in hydrotherapy you lie laughing weakly in the braided waters. Even more precocious machines would make love and earn a living for you, figure your taxes and calories, fight your wars, watch "Bonanza" for you. It seemed especially bad about the wars, since they provide the married man his only real chance to get out of the house for any length of time without a lot of stupid alibis.

Twice I staged half-hearted comebacks in the blackjack contest, but there was not the faintest question about where the real power lay. I don't say the thing cheated, but I won't eliminate the possibility. If the thing is smart enough to work at Cape Canaveral and Oak Ridge it's smart enough to tickle a card off the bottom of the deck.

Bappity-bap, a 6 for me. And a 9. I stood pat.

Bappity-bop, a King for the thing, followed by the inevitable ace. It made a curious noise, as of oily lips smacking. I began to detest it with increasing sincerity.

It sniggered.

It is a repulsive, arrogant, button-infested monster when you get to know it and it is affected into the bargain. "Bad show," it kept saying. God knows where it picked that up or what it reads in its spare time when Munn and the college kids are abed.

I typed, "Knock off the phony British crud."

"That is not in my vocabulary."

You couldn't insult it.

Three more students came in, two girls and a boy. They wanted to know what they'd made on a test, and after Munn had told them they stood around for a while, watching blankly. One of the girls said she'd learned a strange thing—that she could polish patent-leather pumps with a hot biscuit and that on the nights the cafeteria served biscuits she always wore her pumps. She said you just broke open the biscuit and rubbed it over the leather. The other girl said she saw an AP Wirephoto of a monkey cleaning the teeth of a hippopotamus and that you would think it would look nasty, but it seemed natural. Finally the boy student took the arm of each girl and kind of dragged them out, smiling apologetically at Munn and at me and finally at the brain.

When they were gone the machine shook itself down

in its square-cornered skin and asked briskly if I wanted a card. All the worst noises come from the mouthpiece, the typewriter, which now conveyed contempt and what I can describe only as evil amusement: perhaps the latter because of the hot biscuit, but I think not.

"No card," I typed back. "And may all your children strangle on the theory of relativity."

"That's kind of a pun," said Munn without enthusiasm.

The brain suddenly began whining and bumpity-bumping. "That is not in. . . ."

I jogged a key which prevented its telling about its impoverished vocabulary. My wish was to belt it in both accumulators, upper and lower, to sprinkle snuff in the command register and plunge a couple of thumbs into those bleeding lucite buttons. I smiled stiffly at Munn, thanked him for his time and trouble, and headed for the door. As I seized the doorknob the brain hissed me.

Munn said he heard nothing at all, but I know a hiss when I hear one.

The Silent
House

THE CAR BRAKED SMOOTHLY IN FRONT OF THE FRATER-
nity house at the foot of the hill which is the Washington
and Lee University campus. On the hill you saw through
the heavy leaves of the trees the brick buildings and
white columns of the school and halfway up the slope
the corroded bronze statue of Cyrus McCormick, glaring
eternally above a hollow green beard. A quarter-century
ago I'd climbed up there and tunked Cyrus the way you
do a watermelon to see if he was hollow, and discovered
that he was.

This was my first trip back to Lexington (Virginia)

and I felt eager and somehow intimidated, my ears buzzing from seventeen hours of steady driving. I stood a
minute in the front yard of the three-story fraternity
house. The door was open and finally I strolled inside.
I'd tell the kids I just wanted to gawk around, to see my
old room and maybe look at the rug in the lounge where
Joe Walker and I used to pitch quarters for keeps, back
there when a quarter was worth keeping. It would buy
enough gas for Tom Smith's Auburn roadster to swish all
the way to Roanoke.

But there wasn't a sound in the place now. Not a
whisper. The house was filled with the debris of exhaustion, empty beer cans in the hedges, cardboard cartons
in the rooms filled with old test papers, chewed-looking
tennis balls, odd socks and the curled remains of cheese
sandwiches. In my old nest on third the mattress was
rolled back on the springs and a crust of rye bread lay
on the desk beside a gutted ball-point pen.

Down the hall in the corner room where Ed Jelstrup
and Carl Fox had had their fistfight, I half expected to
find traces of that historic disagreement; but it was no
different from the other rooms, no bloodstains, just a
mangled knit tie hanging from a light fixture. Jelstrup
was a transfer from the University of Edinburgh and
he wore heavy brogans with elegant freckles on them.
Most of us pledges would have risked death for a pair of
those freckled shoes but he let it be known, casually, they
were made in Scotland and you had to go there to get
them.

Now I moved into the hallway and called foolishly:
"Hey, fellas, anybody home?" The floor was covered with
peeling linoleum. It had been gleaming hardwood in my

youth. "Hey, fellas!" Not so much as an echo from the plastered walls, one section of which appeared finger-painted with hot-dog mustard.

It was hot in the corridor, the first week of June, almost suffocating. I was on my way to cover a magazine assignment and had told Mary I would stop off at Lexington just for laughs. The place struck me, for all its three stories, as being smaller than I recalled. The really terrible thing about the years is the way they dilute things. When I was a sixteen-year-old freshman the house was formidable. I remembered wandering through endless corridors trying to hide the bottle-green fedora my mother made me wear off to college, searching for a trash basket, the acne itching and stinging on new-shaven jaws, one section of pimples shaped like the state of Florida with maroon lumps for all the principal cities and a yellow one for the capital. The amused glances of wealthy boys from Carolina, Vermont, New York. Rangy and relaxed, "Kid, you brought that hat all the way from Louisiana, you don't want to chunk it *away*."

Sweating now, I thumped downstairs and knocked on the door which had been Mrs. Lee's. She used to be housemother. I beat on the door, suddenly almost sick. Whatever had become of her? She had showed me my first piece of supercivilized cheese and taught me to spread it without exploding the cracker. "Yes, son, that's mold, but you *eat* it, you don't *pick* at it." And there was the night I knocked on this door a long time ago, long before penicillin, and told her I believed I had a fever; and fainted dead away at her feet making (she said later) odd gurgling noises in my strep throat. Where was she? And all the rest of them?

The Fox brothers, who actually faintly resembled beautifully groomed foxes and wore golfing knickers weekends; Billy Carter, the baby-faced boxer; Julius Something, whose father was a judge in St. Louis and who had a theory that egg whites pulled the pus out of pimples. His room reeked of the remedy and of spilled cider¡

A thin Negro in a white jacket materialized in the foyer. "What's the matter, man?" he said. "They ain't nobody here, they gone home for the summer."

I wiped my face and smiled at him. "I used to live here."

"Fine," he said. "That's fine." The tone you use with children when you wish to be rid of them without startling or hurting them.

"I lived here a long time ago, Mrs. Lee was here then."

He shrugged. "Well, I got to clean this place up, it's a fright."

"She had little bitty feet and when she laughed it was the next thing to music." I headed out of the house, toward the waiting car moving through the strangely shrunken foyer, out of a door lower and narrower than it had once been.

"You come back," the man called after me. "You come back when everybody's here."

Lethal
Legend
of Truck-Stop
Food

I HATE TO SHATTER ANY PART OF THE AMERICAN dream, but there are some things one must do as a matter of principle. I feel compelled, therefore, to report the destruction of the warm legend that truck drivers congregate at all the better roadside eating establishments, and that if you want to find good food you would do well to follow suit. I have completed a long and painful 1,200-mile round trip between Hattiesburg, Mississippi, and Oklahoma City. In the course of this long journey I ate at twenty truck stops, drank coffee in perhaps fifty and inspected another thirty or so. I can now disclose with authority and dismay the real facts about the eating habits of truck drivers.

The bitter truth is that a truck driver eats where he can find room to park a tractor-trailer unit which may measure almost sixty feet in length. His meals, generally speaking, are concocted by fine, conscientious people who are good at their trade. Their trade consists of taking the chill off food and placing it in a plate in such a way that it will not fall off onto the floor. Cooking does not appear to be among their responsibilities or accomplishments.

The notion that truck drivers flock naturally to tasty food and superior coffee probably was implanted originally by John Steinbeck in his novel *The Grapes of Wrath*. Steinbeck acknowledged the presence of flies in truck-stop cafés, but they were interesting flies, drawn bigger and brighter than real-life ones, and he never really laid it on the line about the grub. He implied, without drawing the picture too sharply, that the food in these places was simple and honest and stuck to the ribs. What he did not say was that it also sticks to the teeth and the memory.

If there is a universal food for truck drivers it is potato salad, which is made with half-raw potatoes, store-bought mayonnaise and various other odds and ends, the odder the better. I ate potato salad with slivers of green pepper in it, with chunks of celery, with traces of parsley and onion and with scraps of pimento. All of these extras seem to have a fatal appeal to the imagination, or haste, of the truck-stop cook. At one Mississippi truck stop I was able to keep a straight face while asking for the recipe. It developed that the family which owned and operated the café did not wish to make public such a valuable formula. The recipe has been a grim family secret for years. It was impossible to swallow the stuff without a chaser and even after you managed it there were repercussions, strings of tiny, steady hiccups which sounded like marbles falling into a ukulele.

In Louisiana the truck driver is confronted as always with potato salad, but he has a choice, too, of French-type cooking. The trouble is that by the time this cuisine is filtered through the mystique of a truck-stop kitchen it would flatten a tree. The shrimp gumbo, for example, contains green strings of powdered sassafras root. It is perfectly true that these are softer than catgut but they are also much more impervious to moisture.

There is a quaint little place in northern Louisiana, nestled cozily in a tangle of diesel-fuel pumps where you may secure ham and lye hominy swimming in red-eye gravy. As a supper it is discouraging, but it will not make you sick. If this strikes you as a dim compliment it may be because you are not a truck driver with a ten-hour drive ahead of you.

The fare is even more exotic on some of the secondary roads of the Deep South where truck-stop cooks are not faced with the problems of mass production. At one place where I stopped in Louisiana a driver may dine on cold coon casserole, collard greens and a glass of clabber served at room temperature.

In Cooterville, Louisiana, a Mr. Hayes McDole, who formerly operated a truck-stop restaurant, summed up the whole situation with simple eloquence, "Truck drivers," he said soberly, "are not fussy." Mr. McDole now breeds Appaloosa horses, which may be a natural progression from feeding truck drivers.

There is a great deal of rice and gravy served at truck stops throughout Louisiana and in adjacent portions of Texas. Two kinds of gravies predominate, both innocent of meat juice. There is cream gravy, made by browning flour in shortening and then stirring in milk, and brown gravy in which water is substituted for the milk. In either case the result is lethal, capable of burning to a cinder the heart of an adult Indian elephant.

Outside Dallas I ate what was billed as a western-style, chicken-fried steak, swamped in brown gravy. You would think that the meat in Texas, where they grow it, would be excellent, truck-stop cooking notwithstanding. Not so. My steak did not lie flat on the plate like most pieces of meat. At one end of it there was a knob of gristle shaped very much like the heel of a cowboy boot. I thought perhaps it was a freak cut, but in time discovered the truck driver who sat next to me had its identical twin, flanked with pinto beans and creamed potatoes, the same as mine.

At Texas truck stops they chicken-fry practically everything—eggplant, veal, shrimp and even chickens. The Southern Fried Chicken extends far into Oklahoma and possibly farther, heaven forbid. The eateries use cracker crumbs or plain bread crumbs to produce a crust on animal or vegetable. Even the elusive okra is robbed of its mobility, skid-proof in the stern clasp of the mixture. It comes to you formless and golden without a wiggle in it. You strike a chicken leg and the crust falls away in a curved sheet to disclose a sight best forgotten.

Somewhere before you reach Oklahoma the rice-and-gravy dish ends, though the potato salad and other stuff lingers on. At Marietta, Oklahoma, a female cook, pondering the idea of mixing rice with gravy, produced these words, "I don't say that it couldn't be *done*—but I wouldn't *do* it." In Oklahoma the potato reigns as unquestioned sovereign of the truck-stop café. Near Ardmore I followed a cheerful-looking red pickup truck loaded with bales of hay into the parking area of a restaurant which offered hash-browned, French-fried, creamed and boiled potatoes. I was told that if I'd arrived an hour earlier I could also have ordered potatoes with molten cheese.

If one sought to establish himself as a kind of Duncan Hines of the truck stops he could issue few, if any, seals of total approval. I encountered three broad classifications of food. Reading from best to worst, they were: 1) not enjoyable, 2) endurable, and 3) survivable. Several truckers spoke wistfully of a sort of super truck terminal at Wichita Falls, Texas, where a Texaco sign sticks up fifty feet in the air and the eating is out of this world, but Wichita Falls was off my route and I can only report hearsay.

It is possible that if I had had the time and the constitution to prolong the investigation, other good places would have come to light. Meantime my only regret is that I had but one duodenum to give for my curiosity.

Joe Rumsey, who drives for Viking Lines out of Memphis, says that as long as truckers must eat where they can find parking space there is no ready solution. Joe drives a big rig, an interstate, motor-freight job. Some weeks he makes as much as $200. He is a quiet, tired man who says that because he is never able to find what he wants to eat on the road "I'm always about half-hungry."

I stopped at several country grocery stores where parking space was adequate for a tractor-trailer. It developed that there are certain rogue drivers who go on binges of eating canned foods, forsaking the fellowship of their kind and ignoring the cafés for days on end. These boys, one store owner said, "favor pink foods"— Vienna sausage, boiled ham, corned beef and the like. Yet there is no hard and fast rule in this renegade group. My informant also said he has one customer who never buys anything but soda crackers and buttermilk.

America has the wrong idea about its truck drivers. These men are not the nonconforming, rough-talking ladies' men of legend—independent, cocky and gay. The gray truth is that the modern truck driver is a different breed altogether, lonely and brooding for the most part, given to staring at his blackeyed peas and walking off without eating them. Strict Interstate Commerce Commission regulations have taken their toll of some of the old crowd. No doubt cream gravy and potato salad have done for the rest. They say, after all, that it was a shortage of proper food that finally knocked off the dinosaur.

It's hard to know where the blame lies for all this. A truck stop worthy of the name operates twenty-four hours a day, with three shifts of waitress-cook teams, often only one man and woman to the team. They do what they can in the time allotted. They do not ask high praise. They are pathetically grateful if a trucker finishes his meal and says in a tone of mild surprise, "Hey, that wasn't *bad*." Their hours are poor and the pay is the same.

Contrary to a widely held belief, truck drivers are not compulsive tippers. They *are* compulsive worriers about the occupational hazards of their craft. "Them tractors shake a man to pieces," an Oklahoma waitress told me. She waved a disgusted hand at a display case which contained—in addition to lighter fluid, flashlights and pocket combs—three different brands of digestive aids, a stick to treat chapped lips, some tablets to prevent dozing, and two kinds of aspirin. She shrugged and raised peanut-butter-colored eyebrows, "So what am I, a *doctor?*"

As we talked, a driver punched a coin into the jukebox and stood there in the corner of the room glowering at the spinning record. I later learned that he had rolled a rig into a ditch a few days earlier. You could still see the scabbed cuts on his jaw and she called out to him, "Hey, Joe, you look like you been sacking wildcats and run out of sacks right in the middle of it."

Ah, I thought, this was it at last, a glimmer of the classic truck-stop talk—tough and tender, rough words masking depths of sympathy, perhaps camouflaging one of those stealthy, sinewy romances in the Steinbeck manner, in which the very copper rivets of the driver's blue jeans glow with symbolism and leashed desire. I waited for the driver's answer.

"You got any Juicy Fruit?" he said.

Once
I Was
a Tiger

FOR YEARS I HAVE TOYED WITH THE IDEA OF RETURNING to Fort Benning, Ga., a quarter as big as Rhode Island, geared to its paratroops, a place where 18 years and 50 pounds ago I learned the manly art of leaping from an aircraft in fright. Now by what seems a vague miracle involving a few telephone calls and an exchange of letters with the Defense Department and various public information offices, I am back for a visit to this encampment, one of the richest wellsprings of an incurable nostalgia.

In the time when I sweated through jump school,

parachuting had not been accepted generally as a sport and no one foresaw a day when pretty stenographers wearing gung-ho bras beneath fluorescent coveralls would spend Sundays sky-diving just for gasps and giggles. I am pleased to discover anew at Benning that military jumping is masculine, dead serious. (I quickly rediscover, too, that it is painful.) I already have permission to jump from the short practice tower, and have been told that the Information Officer is working on the general to clear me for the 250-foot tower and—apogee of delight—from an actual plane.

But first, fitted out in borrowed fatigues and boots, I am to have a taste of what nowadays is described as physical conditioning and motivation. My mentor during this journey down memory lane is to be Sgt. Vincent Becker, a jumpmaster and veteran of more than 300 jumps. It is a new assignment for him and he does not relish it, but as we arrive at the rope-climbing pit he says without bitterness, "We'll have to try to get you in *some* kind of shape. Honest, you don't look ready to jump out of a *taxi.*"

I shrug and seize one of the dangling 25-foot ropes and begin climbing. The rope is thick as a man's wrist, and when I am eight feet above the sawdust I know I am finished. I have the will to climb higher, but I am out of gasoline and I cling there like a lost lemur. I experience a lonely aching in the armpits and an intense desire to sneeze. I cannot release the rope to jam a finger under my nose, but finally I manage to squirm around and get the rope against my upper lip. This is good because it quells the itch in my nose and I know if I sneeze I shall turn loose and crash.

Sergeant Becker says, "For Godsake don't eat it, Pops, *climb* it."

I begin inching downward. The rope burns and smells of sweat, but I do not complain because this is what I asked for. I say to Becker, "I used to go all the way to the top."

Becker, who can do push-ups on one hand, makes an earnest effort to seem impressed.

After a time we plod over to another sawdust pit, this one rimmed with stubby wooden platforms and Becker demonstrates the 1963 version of the parachute-landing fall. The body must shift in the direction of fall, a kind of skier's twist of bent knees. We used to go limp and tumble, and trust to luck and ligaments. After Becker is finished I try a series of falls, but until now I haven't fallen down in years. The last time was on the ice in front of a Chinese restaurant in Denver. Becker is obviously depressed by what he sees.

Time after wretched time the sawdust soars up in a sheet and whacks the side of my head and I lie there spent and itching, gazing into the cold, blue Georgia sky. I am beginning to be sick to my stomach.

Becker helps me to my feet. "You want to rest?"

"No, I'm fine."

"You don't look fine," he says.

I begin to think there are serious, if not fatal, flaws in my plan for revisitation.

Behind a training platoon we flop down and do some push-ups. Becker says we must be careful not to call attention to ourselves because it may demoralize the trainees to see me lying on my face after only a few exertions.

§ 226 §

Up-down, up-down, the kids keep pushing up, fresh as pistons. When they stand up they roar: "AIRBORNE!" Rarely does the minute pass you don't hear one group or another in the area hollering "AIRBORNE!" It comes from the 250-foot towers, from the swing-landing trainer, from the wind machine and from the airstrip where fourth-weekers are loading into the planes. It occurs to me to ask Becker why no one hollers "GERONIMO!" any more but I do not wish to appear petulant about the changes. Nothing is the same—the planes are different, the parachutes are larger and olive-colored instead of white, the jump-commands are altered. Everything.

It is not at all as I had hoped. It is no showcase for ancient skills. I fail to make a decent exit from the door of a mock-up plane, using the outdated shuffle, kicking out with the wrong foot and doing a half-turn in the air. Becker is embarrassed. To explain matters, he tells the instructor, "F.D.R. was President when he came through jump school."

I try it a half dozen more times and finally it is plain to all concerned that I am strictly from Geronimo and if we stay there all night in the dusty dummy plane it is not going to be any different.

Becker leads me to my car. I am a mass of hurt. Tomorrow we will tackle the 34-foot tower and if I'm ever going to, I'll recapture the feeling of the thing. After that, the big tower and the plane. The thought of it is beginning to reach me. Maybe the clearance won't come through.

That night, in my room at the tourist court, I begin to feel, for the first time, a little chicken. I call my wife

long distance. She wants to know if they are going to let me jump from a plane.

"It's awfully silly. It's really silly at your age," she says. "I hope they won't let you."

I could squeeze her. She echoes my sentiments to the syllable. I am chicken, as cheerfully chicken as Henny Penny.

Becker meets me at 7:45 A.M. and we go straight to the tower to have done with it. The tower is the last place in Georgia I want to go but I figure if I face up to it, it will be finished in a matter of minutes.

An instructor fits me into harness on the ground at the foot of the tower. My metal fasteners clink as we climb the zigzag stairs up to the crest. High above us I hear someone sing out: "TIGER!" And then, a chorus: "A-ggh-rrr-r!"

"What's that?"

Becker shrugs. "We had better keep moving. We can't clog the works."

When we reach the top, there is the devil's own racket. Trainees are stomping toward the jump-doors like Spanish dancers imitating horses. This is the new way. I stomp in imitation, feeling foolish, as if I have a rose in my teeth. "Not bad," says Becker alongside me. "But you got the wrong foot in front."

Standing in the door I try not to look down, but my eyes are drawn to the heads of the trainees waiting in line below. Their helmets look no bigger than beans. I hold the sides of the door and lean backward, feeling that the noise and movement will shake me out into emptiness before I am ready. "Remember to duck your head," my instructor-sergeant says.

"TIGER!" yells the instructor. I do not, I cannot, growl.

"You scared?" the instructor asks. "Becker tells me that you're an old trooper."

I lie: "I'm not scared."

"Get ready!"

"I'm ready."

He slaps me on the rump and out I sail like a wild goose and I hear the trolley overhead zizzing on the cable. Seconds later it is over and I ask Becker, "How was it?"

"Pretty bad," he says.

"I do something wrong?"

"Just about everything." He is unbuckling the dummy reserve chute on my chest to get at the harness. "You crossed your hands on the reserve like you had the cramps, your exit was weak and you turned completely around in the air like you were trying to climb back in the tower."

Nevertheless the orange dirt feels dandy beneath the soles of the borrowed boots. It is great dirt, of a fine solidity. Off to the north, in the cold blue sky, I see a string of jumpers spill from a fat C-119, dark specks falling, then the flat mushrooms of olive nylon shimmering in descent, swinging. The sight is a beautiful and proud one, but it saddens me. I really hope the general decides not to let me jump. Back in 1944 I was mad at the Japs, but I'm not mad at anyone at all now.

As I am resting, Becker asks, "You really used to be a jumper? No fooling?"

I reach in a pocket and fish out my old Parachute School certificate, dated Dec. 1, 1944 and signed by Brig. General Ridgely Gaither. The certificate is folded in

§ 230 §

quarters and it is split and yellowing. "Well," Becker says, "that's really something."

On the obstacle course next morning I scramble halfway through a metal culvert and lie down to think. The iron is cool against my cheek and there is a wonderful privacy in the dull green light. Becker is waiting for me to crawl out the other end.

He has news for me. He says, as if he is handing me a prize package of some sort, that it will be all right for me to go off the 250-foot towers. While I was in the culvert, the judge advocate's office delivered a waiver for me to sign, promising that if I fracture anything or cease breathing I will not prosecute the government. I read the waiver nervously and sign. I ask him how I can prosecute if I am deceased.

We go over to the big towers, which have not changed in the years; they are like oil well derricks, with four arms extending from the crown, a circle of steel beneath the tip of each arm and a canopy spread inside each circle, a man hanging beneath each canopy.

Becker says, "You ready to go, Pops?"

"Go?"

"You ready to go up?"

I say to Becker, "Let's save this till later, you know, a little later." I try to grin. "It will be a kind of dessert."

"Whatever you say." He stares thoughtfully at me.

A lieutenant is bustling toward us, waving a clipboard. When he is near us, he slows pace and says, "They're going to let the writer jump."

I rub my face, unbelieving. "From a plane?"

"Yes," the lieutenant says. He is glad for me.

There is little conversation on the way to the airstrip and less while I am being harnessed in the sweat shed. The day has darkened and you can hear the wind on the walls of the shed, scraping under the eaves. Aircraft motors grumble and cough outside on the strip. The harness is so snug that when I try to take a deep breath a strap bites me in two.

Sergeant Becker accompanies me into the plane, where 36 trainees are waiting in full equipment to make their fifth, and qualifying, jump. I ride hunched and wordless in the tail, contemplating my fate. I feel strangled and doomed, and suspect I shall never again see another fried egg in my kitchen at home. Soft and angerless, I shall leap into the wind, a sacrifice to nostalgic doodling.

Suddenly Becker materializes in the gloom, holding on to the static line anchor-cable. Beside him stands Colonel Mike Paulick, who heads Airborne-Air Mobility. "Ceiling's gray cotton down to 1,100 feet, closing fast," Becker says. "It's called off. We'll jump early in the morning. It should clear by then."

"Go ahead and tell him," the colonel smiles.

Becker says, "The colonel wasn't going to let you jump anyway. The general says you have to have written permission from the Department of Defense. You have to write them a letter and they have to mail an affirmative. It takes a long time."

I frowned. "How long?"

"Cut it out," Becker says.

I stand up, cut by the straps but thrilled. They really aren't going to let me do it. They won't even hear of it. We file from the plane with the trainees, down onto the concrete, which is firm and sane and doesn't have that I'm-going-up vibration of the plane.

Becker unbuckles me, disarms me, lifts off more than 60 pounds of equipment. As we are saying goodbye, he asks to see my Parachute School certificate again. He looks at it for a while and hands it back to me. "I'll be damned," he says.

That night I head for home. I will mail no request to the Department of Defense. I do not trust them to remain unresponsive.

O Lost
and by
the Gin
Grieved

MY FAMILY HAS BEEN GONE FOR A WEEK AND THE
kitchen does not resemble anything one might expect
this side of the moon. The sink, half-filled with aged
water and clotted dishes and pots, is rimed with ridges of
different kinds of mold, curiously lunar in appearance,
neither fluid nor solid, green nor blue, an unearthly compromise of texture and tint, possessed of an odor not
sweet nor yet an honest stink, enough to unstring the
nerves and set the senses reeling.

I swing open the refrigerator door and strands of

§ 234 §

vintage spinach (probably June 7, 1962) swing like wind-chimes from the underside of the meat-tray beneath the ice-freezing compartment. The spinach suffers no inde-cision in color or texture. It is black as the inside of a mule and tough as whipleather. I tug a string of it and it does not break or come loose from its mooring, the tray sliding outward with the pulling. Inside the tray is perhaps a third of an inch of bloody water and in the water are two chops. The only reason they are recogniz-able as chops is because Mary said that was what they were before she took the children to Alexandria, Louisi-ana, to visit relatives.

A half-used can of chili reposes on a wire shelf im-mediately beneath the tray and chops. There is no lid on the can of chili. The greases have congealed in orange circles.

My pulse quickens, for there in the plastic nests molded inside the main door of the refrigerator are three eggs, wonderfully clean in the carnage. One sees at a glance that the eggs in their fine natural containers, bloodless, greaseless and innocent of chemical preserva-tive or artificial coloring, are more than food. They are dear and familiar symbols of sanity, of those distant days when you simply sat down at a table and forked and chewed and swallowed.

But when these eggs are knocked against the rim of a skillet they do not make the noise *skrish*. They make the noise *thuck*. They are frozen and it is like hammer-ing the skillet with a golfball. Nevertheless, they can be boiled. A simple but excellent supper may be made of three soft-boiled eggs, crisp buttered toast and scalding, fragrant coffee. I have never really liked coffee, but when

I think of it as scalding and fragrant it doesn't seem too bad. Perhaps I could take all of it out on the back steps and eat in the open air, musing there among the fireflies, forgetting the kitchen and the rest of the stricken house.

I bring the water to a racing boil and turn on the oven for the toast. I find the butter in a saucer in the refrigerator. What butter there is is of a baguette shape, approximately the size of the Hope Diamond. This is large for a diamond but not very big for butter. It is streaked with ketchup and mustard and something I could not, and cannot, describe. When the family departed it was plain yellow, but it is clear now that this has been a very busy piece of butter the past seven days. It glitters sickeningly.

Actually there is no need for toast. I think of the peoples of China, many of whom have never laid eyes on a piece of toast, dry or buttered. I recall the half-starved Japanese in 1947, wearing their lunches to work, pitiful flat cans of boiled rice and seaweed strapped to the small of the back with a cloth sash. My eyes sting as I remember the way they licked the last grains of rice from the corners of the cans.

What *they* wouldn't have given for three softboiled eggs and a swallow of honest coffee!

When the water is boiling I drop in the frozen eggs and they go off like depth bombs, exploding one by one, putting out tentacles, quills and nubbins of white: lumps, question marks and knots. A brownish foam forms with merciful swiftness on the surface of the water, obscuring the bobbling mess.

I had planned to use the same boiling water to make the coffee.

This, then, was supper.

§ 236 §

I drooled the entire mess into the kitchen garbage can, which is the kind that opens its mouth when you step on its foot. It had bad breath and I got off the pedal as quickly as possible.

If the breath of the garbage can is any index of what I've been eating since the family left me, it is marvelous that I am still alive.

This line of conjecture sets off a new trend of thinking, stoking to life a fear that has ridden me for some time, the fear of dying alone and unheeded. Frequently it comes over me in hotel and motel rooms, when I am alone on the road. As long as it takes to secure a bucket of ice or a club sandwich in a hotel, there is no telling how many weeks one might spend unattended, unloved, indeed *unburied.* A friend of mine who is a police radio-dispatcher says that the terror of solitary death is not an uncommon neurosis and that one old lady phones him two or three nights a week to ask for a police check on her place. Sometimes she imagines there is a bleeding body in the attic and that the blood is coming down through the ceiling and this, far from alarming her, she seems to find exhilarating. She is sincerely tickled that someone else has died before she did, says my friend.

I find a piece of gum in my pocket and chew the sweet juice out of it, drinking a glass of water, glancing at the kitchen ceiling before snapping out the light. The gum is agreeable but not filling, and I resist the impulse to swallow it.

In the dining room I remember the bottle of Beefeater's gin in the kitchen cupboard and I go back into the kitchen and pour a drink into a cheese glass. The taste of the raw drink is not good and I feel evil, standing there

alone with the stuff in my hand. There is a cheap mirror on the wall between the windows and I stare self-pityingly into rippled glass, the lobe of one ear stretching longer than the other, the face red and blurred, the sly raddled features of the abandoned drunkard.

The hole in the sink swallows the rest of the gin at a gulp. I may be hungry and starved for the sound of a familiar voice, but I'm damned if I shall die here reeking of drink. I can hear Wilhelm Pollett down at Pollett's Funeral Home saying "The poor son of a bitch must have starting sucking the bottle the minute his family got out the front *door*." Pollett once told me in an uncharacteristic moment of confidence that many middle-aged men depart the ranks of the living while trying to be gay in the absence of loved ones. These fellows, after years, even decades of cautious living, suddenly seek to rend great chunks from the meat of life and not infrequently it chokes them. Pollett told me there was only one worse thing for a man in his forties, and that was to awaken in the middle of the night and decide on serious business with a female, even if she happened to be his wife. "An older man's system can't *adjust* suddenly from sleep to all *that*." No telling how many middle-agers died wearing only the tops of their pajamas, Pollett said. And these made the "tiredest looking" corpses of all.

There is a navy blue sock with an armored-looking toe on the dining-room table. I brush the sock onto the floor and set up the typewriter and begin working, figuring to go out later and get a sandwich or some doughnuts and milk.

The cooling house creaks and cracks and now I have the feeling that someone or something is standing in the doorway staring at the back of my neck. The skin contracts warmly, then cools and prickles and the small hairs stiffen in rows, starting just above the collar and moving in waves to the base of the skull. This is silly and I refuse to stop and look behind me. I think of Chris, sensible and without pretense. Chris would have looked right off the bat and then either he would have screamed and fled, or, perceiving nothing in the doorway, relaxed.

It must be ten o'clock and there are no lights on at the Traubs' house next door, nor is there any sound from the Joneses on the other side. I would even welcome a blast from young Peter Jones' untamed bugle which, when he plays it, sounds somehow blasphemous and submerged. I can *feel* the dark strings of spinach swinging in the airless cold of the refrigerator, and what is worse, I sense the somber working of the mold in the sink and the tightening of timbers throughout this rotten old house in which countless dozens have lived and laughed and suffered and died.

I stop typing, listening. A click, a low growling and trickling. I whirl and look at the doorway and there, slope-shouldered and still, is the jacket I hangered and suspended from the wooden facing an hour earlier. Behind it, in the boys' bedroom, darkness. My stomach growls again and this time I know it for what it is and imagine the searching, puzzled digestive acids probing all the empty wrinkles and deciding, well, the hell with it, the bastard must have cut his throat.

I go to the phone. A week is long enough. "Operator, hello operator, I want to call Alexandria, no, in Louisiana not Virginia. . . ."

No More
Music

Intermelodic Record Club
Office of the Collection Mgr.
Malamute, Ill.

Elliott Chaze
1013 West Pine St.
Mattiesburg, Miss.

Dear Member:
Our Accounting Department has filed with us for collection your long-past-due account.

§ 241 §

Although periodic statements and reminders have been sent to you, without result, it is our fervent wish to help you keep favorable your credit standing. To do this we urge you to send your payment for the balance shown at the bottom of this page.

Without further DELAY!

This will facilitate our clearing your credit record and return your account to topflight standing—a course we favor to the alternative of *drastic* collection measures.

We value your goodwill and friendship. Please send the payment now, in the enclosed envelope.

Respectfully,
Clemmons Tongsley
Collection Mgr.

Elliott Chaze
1013 West Pine St.,
Hattiesburg, Miss.

Mr. Clemmons Tongsley, Collection Mgr.
Intermelodic Record Club
Malamute, Ill.

Dear Sir:

To begin with, may I request that in future you cease addressing correspondence to me in care of the city of Mattiesburg, Miss. The name of the town is funny enough the way it really is. The place is Hattiesburg, it was named after the founder's wife. City records establish clearly that no one ever called her Mattie. Her name was Hattie and I am grateful that it was not Hattie Belle, or Hattie Mae or Hattie Lee in the Southern tradition because I could not bear to have friends write me at any more comical address than this one. There are worse names, of course. There is a Trussville in Alabama and a Wartburg in Tennessee.

As for your bill, which lists:

Grieg Schumann	BC	1080	6	$6.51
Schubert Sym 9	MS	6219	8	6.51
Tchai Swn Lake	KS	6308	6	7.54
Strav Firebird	MS	6328	7	6.51

TOTAL NOW DUE
$27.07

I did not order Tchai Swn Lake, Strav Firebird or any of the others. As for Tchai Swn Lake there was not even a record in the little slot when finally I got past the mud-colored corrugated paper shell. On the inside it was beautiful, a glossy folder, mostly in slick browns and pinks, both of which colors are among my favorites. Margot Fonteyn stood on the clenched toes of her right foot (a fact that fascinated my youngest daughter Jecca) and a man with great pink calves and ruffles at his wrists was holding her steady, her left leg high in a ballet position which my late Uncle Jim used to call, kiddingly, la-poot. You would have liked him. He had a name for everything and he was the only oilfield driller I ever knew who actually bit off a man's ear in a fight.

There was a masterfully written history of Tchaikovsky's composition of *The Sleeping Beauty Ballet.* When the director of the Imperial Theaters at St. Petersburg (Alexander Vsevolozhsky) suggested the idea the composer was charmed, it says in the liner. But like I say, there wasn't a sign of a record in the slot and you have billed me $7.54 for a rather short story about a man in whom I would have no interest even if he were alive, and whose music I am too ignorant to understand or appreciate. I would not trade a decent record of "Stardust" for everything Tchai ever did, including Swn Lake KS 6308 6 7.54 in spades. I haven't the faintest idea about the KS or the 6308 or the 6, but assume they're all hooked up with Tchai in this flood of symbolic gobbledygook which has confounded me ever since I became a member of the Intermelodic Record Club. You people throw numbers around as if they grow on trees and you never explain them. If you ask me, numbers are pretty serious things and never were intended to be squirted across the page as carelessly as you are inclined to squirt them.

I have talked with a half-dozen other members of Intermelodic and they don't understand the numbers either; and four of them admitted that they shared my general frustration and no longer bothered to try to order the records they really liked. They simply let the things come each month and pay for them, because it is simpler than trying to check all the little choice-cards and read the suggestion lists.

One friend said he'd gotten Stravinsky's *Firebird* three times and all he ever really wanted was "Harvest Moon," which hasn't come yet.

The only reason I ever got into this at all was because a fellow reporter who has been having a very hard time came to me and said if he could sign me up as a new member Intermelodic would give him, free of charge, three or four new records. I felt sorry for him because he limps in bad weather and also because he had to have his gall bladder removed and some kind of surgery on his Common Duct almost finished him last winter. He said I could sign as either a classic, or popular music member, but that it didn't make any difference in the long run. I understand now what he meant by its not making any difference. I keep getting records I never heard of and when I write that I want out of the club, no one bothers to answer me.

Well, sir, I still want out.

I will pay the bill on one condition. The reason I haven't already paid it is that every time I send you a check, here comes another batch of Beethoven or Bach or Tchai (I've got the latter running out of my ears, even subtracting the Tchai that wasn't in the slot when I opened it). The condition on which I'll pay the bill is that you state in writing that if I do you will not send me any more records.

This seems a fair enough swap if you mean it about wanting my goodwill and friendship.

Let me quote from the back of the *Firebird Ballet* (Complete) folder, in the words of Igor Stravinsky:

"The Firebird did not attract me as a subject. Like all 'story' ballets, it demanded 'descriptive' music of a kind I did not want to write. . . ."

Stravinsky did not even want to *write* it.

And I assure you I don't want to *receive* it, much less *listen* to it.

Sincerely yours,
Elliott Chaze

§ 245 §

The Case
of the Throttling
Underpants

EVER SINCE I CAN REMEMBER THERE HAS BEEN THIS
shortage of underwear pants and it seems that no matter
how many pairs I buy the situation persists in one degree
or another, this despite the fact that my modest wardrobe
bursts at the seams with T-shirts of all sizes, ages and
colors. I am perhaps owner of the only banana-colored
T-shirts in this country today and I possess, also, T-shirts
in tones of elderberry, oyster, mockingbird-gray, and
telephone-pole brown. The color of the T-shirts is not a
constant thing, thanks to our home laundry, and a T-

shirt which this week is the exact shade of weathered and creosoted wood may, the following week, after traveling through the washing machine in company with Chris's Christmas-play burnoose, developed a fine purple underflush, presenting now a combination of brown and apoplexy which may be described as company-commander cherry.

The colors, shifting and changing and unpredictable as they are, do not distress me and in summer are a real advantage in that I am in position to instruct a friend, "Meet me in front of Kress's around noon, you won't have any trouble spotting me, I'll be wearing a pink thing with slate-blue shoulders and stomach." But the underpants crisis has hurt me and continues to do so. Once I risked lockjaw because on the day I cut the heel of my hand on a rusty nail in a parking lot I had no underpants on and declined to go to the hospital for a tetanus injection, since these frequently, if not always, are given in the hip. I could have bought a new pair of underpants, but in a small town even the mildest eccentricities cast long shadows and by suppertime it would have been spread all over the place that I went into a store, purchased a pair of drawers and put them on in the dressing-booth; that clearly when I came into the store I wore no drawers whatsoever, or, worse had soiled the old ones and carried them off in my pocket after changing.

You can see that it is not a simple problem and that it can be in truth a perilous one.

This morning, after digging through a fluffy riot of color in the bureau and finding no sign of underwear pants, I sat down on the edge of the bed, wearing only my new loafers and tennis socks and a short T-short the color of a roach that has not been much in the sunshine. Whenever it is necessary for me to look for a lost or misplaced object I become rather dizzy and my eyes feel smaller and closer together. I get tired. Even my fingers and ribs feel exhausted and although I do not wish to die on the instant I have little appetite for living.

Hunched there on the bed I review all the fine pairs of underpants I have owned in twenty-four years of home-laundering: boxer-type shorts with puckered elastic which makes tuck-marks in the flesh of the abdomen, gripper-fastened shorts, shorts with small strings to tie above the hips, jockey-shorts both ribbed and unribbed with handy knitted bags in front and soft as kittens. The latter I ceased wearing when I read that perhaps they made one sterile because they preserved too much body-heat, or something like that; anyway I quit them and never have been able to reconcile the tone of the article with the fact many of the nation's outstanding jockeys have sired children.

Now I arise from the bed and walk into the kitchen, aware of every vagrant draft, but not really caring since the children have gone to schcool and it would serve Mary right to see me this way. I open a drawer beneath the sink where she keeps different kinds of things made of cloth. More than once I've found what I needed here.

Sure enough, there is a pair of underpants and I put them on in the kitchen, holding onto the edge of the round table made of redwood planks. The morning sun streams through the window and, as they say in the sexy books, paints my soft body with interesting shadows from the window fan. There is a long slit in the right side of the seat and I call hoarsely for Mary.

She does not laugh when she sees me standing there. She simply shrugs and registers a look of persecution, as though I have torn out the seat of the shorts with my bare hands.

"Take 'em off," she says. "I'll sew them."

I commence pulling them down and she reconsiders hastily, "Never mind, I'll sew them the way they are—on you. It won't take a second."

She is a seasoned campaigner in the matter of underpants and does not ask a single question about why don't I get another pair out of my drawer. She *knows* there is no other pair. She sews steadily when we are in the bedroom, but I feel that even considering the need for vertical sewing she is abnormally rough, in that she jerks at the material and interferes with my balance. My balance is never much to brag about before nine o'clock in the morning and when I lurch she apologizes but doesn't put her heart into it. I have seen campers sew up a tear in a tent (using a piece of string and a tenpenny nail) more gently than this.

"There," says Mary. "There you are."

"*Thanks.*" I am deliberately sarcastic.

She has a temper of her own, but says nothing. She does not come right out and giggle, but her shoulders shake as she leaves the bedroom and I hear her talking to Marion, the part-time maid, in the kitchen. I go to the door, then return and complete dressing, satisfied they are not discussing my smallclothes.

I've some mailing to do downtown and some other errands and visits and within the hour I know that Mary has sewed with more haste than skill. Somehow she has tightened the right leg of the shorts and there is a stran-

gulation there. In time it becomes more serious and my friend at the registered-mail window remarks that I appear on edge. "Mostly," he says, "you are not the jumpy type, God knows I get enough of the jumpy type, it takes *time* to register these things, you know, to fill out the blanks and specifiy the return receipts, figure up postage for air mail, special delivery, insurance. . . ."

With an effort I tune him out. I wish he would shut up. My right leg seems almost asleep and I stomp the foot on the marble floor.

Joe, the barber, says to me a half-hour later: "You aren't sitting very still, are you?" I have heard him say the same thing to Chris. I am afraid Joc is going to lay down the clippers and reach in the little flat drawer under his glass-faced tool cabinet and get me a piece of bubble gum.

Someone in another chair begins talking baseball, very loudly, and then, when it seems this will never end, everybody starts laughing and laughing, insanely and endlessly, at a joke about a woman who accidentally lays her breast in an ashtray while drinking Martinis at a bar. I am in pain, real pain. The right leg of the underpants apparently has climbed completely up and off the beaten track and now in an ever-tightening burst of secret cruelty, is bent on nothing short of emasculation.

"Let me up," I say. "Let me up, Joe."

"Just a minute," Joe says soothingly. "One minute."

"I can't *wait* a minute."

"Now there," he says, almost in baby talk. "There, there, just let me snip the fuzz out of this ear."

I come out of the chair in a shower of hair and with a great flapping of cloth, seizing my groin, clawing and rending. At the first ripping sound Joe seems startled, but when I continue to tear loose the hidden, strangling fabric, he begins to look frightened. He has seen some strange things in his years of barbering, but I believe this is the first time he ever has watched a customer do anything like this. The room is deadly quiet. There is no more talk of baseball or of the burned nipple in the ashtray, no laughing. In the mirror behind Joe's chair I see the other barbers and customers, all transfixed, like bugs or flowers frozen in a block of clear plastic.

"Ah," I say. "Ah, but that's fine, that's *good* now."

"Sure." Joe's jaw has dropped, and now he resembles a dog squaring off to bite a flea. He laughs weakly. After all, his kindly face seems to say, this fellow has been coming to me a long time and by God if he wants to rip his drawers now and then, who am *I* to criticize?

When he is finished with me and I have paid him he pretends great interest in one of the silver half-dollars I have handed him. He says, by golly, he believes it is a collector's item and he will show it to Mr. Nitney across the street. It is a most ordinary half-dollar and I know Joe will never take it to Nitney, but Joe is a man of enormous tact, and now he is intent on arranging to get me out of the shop feeling as normal as a man can feel after putting on such a strange show.

"You sure you don't want to keep this four-bits?" Joe stares at it, turning it over in his hand.

"No thanks."

"Well," Joe smiles, "I tell you what, if it's a collector's item we'll split the profit—that's what we'll do, you *hear*?"

"Sure."

"You come back, hear?"

"All right." My ears glow like neon all the way home.

I have now been home perhaps an hour and I am in the kitchen after ice water. I drink it out of the cold bottle and as usual it tastes of lipstick and peanut butter and jelly, since everyone uses the bottle and no matter how many times we swear off this practice, there is no change of status. Marion is fumbling around in the drawer under the sink, looking for something, and she shakes her head and mutters, finally dumping the entire contents of the drawer on the redwood table. It cheers me to see someone else looking for something.

Mary enters and Marion says to her, "You seen my dust rag anywhere, the *white* one?"

"Yes, I've seen it."

"Well?"

"I'm afraid you won't be able to use it today," says Mary. "The master of the house is *wearing* it."

The Monkey
That Ate
with
His Feet

BECAUSE I AM BUILT FULL IN THE BARREL AND HAVE
withered hips it is not likely I shall ever find a pair of
pants to fit me right off the rack. Invariably they must
be altered and although they do not fit much better after
alteration I have the feeling that at least a token effort
has been made to bring me and the pants together in the
places where a lack of togetherness is most noticeable.
In gray-flannel slacks which have not been diminished
in the seat the cloth covering my behind slides and yaws
in the manner of the afterskin of an elephant and there
is a rippling and play of shadow which is distracting

even to persons who have known me a long time. When the slack has been removed the pants are tight against my thighs and this has a tendency to wear all the hair off the fronts of my legs, but one cannot have everything. And I am certainly no worse off than Chris, whose pants legs must be chopped at the bottoms no matter how short they are in the beginning, the new cuffs always so wide and gaping they entrap everything he drops and some items he is actually trying to throw away.

These things I mention not with the idea of gaining sympathy for both or either of us, but because they explain how and why Chris and I have become so very much at home in the alterations departments of several stores. A considerable portion of our time is spent trying on pants or waiting for them to be finished, and the women who do the actual work are no longer afraid of us, with or without our pants. They have come to accept the truth that my son and I are not simply cranks who like to lurch around in dressing booths, and that it is no fault of ours that my hips have withered while my belly bloomed or that Chris's legs are barely long enough to reach all the way down to the ground. Some of the women even call us by our first names and this I recognize for the distinction it is because to these hardworking craftsmen most males are little more than a number on a cardboard ticket. Some time ago there was an alterations department seamstress who called us honey but she did not last long and it was just as well since her work was reckless, if not injurious. Some of the cuffs she manufactured for Chris reached midway to his knees, like pirate boots, and the fronts of my thighs shone smooth as glass.

For the most part these women are as fine a lot as

you will find anywhere and although they affect no airs they are far from destitute. I have one graying friend in alterations whose daughter is married to a paratrooper overseas and every summer, regular as July rolls around, this friend sets aside her needle and shears and pops off to Europe as if it were no farther away than New Orleans. Another owns various parcels of real estate and several times has asked me if I had any notion of selling our place on West Pine, a one-storied structure of many gables with anguished flooring that screams beneath the tread of a medium-sized cockroach.

Perhaps the most interesting of all the alterations ladies, day in and day out, mainly because she gives Chris chewing gum and partly because she is the kind of a person things *happen* to, is a mild and articulate one who takes her lunch to work with her in a brown paper bag. It is not only the lunch that fires the imagination, but also the way she *cares* for the *bag*, having used one for a month or more and it looked as good as new and would still be in service if it had not got rained on. I shall give you a sample of one of her days as she told it to Chris and me:

"I was headed for the store at about 8:30 A.M. and I saw this monkey chained to a parking meter on the corner in front of the California Sandwich Shop. You know where that is, they sell the long sandwiches pointed at both ends with seeds on them.

"I didn't look him (the monkey) in the eye. You know how it is, you just don't stare into the eyes of a strange monkey."

Chris interrupted her to ask when we were going downstairs to buy his new shoes.

She smiled in a companionable manner and stroked the top of his head and continued the tale, rubbing his head to keep him quiet, but not offering him a second piece of gum because he had stuck the other piece on the window.

"So really I wasn't paying too much attention to the monkey and then I felt him grab the paper bag, my lunch bag. He pulled so hard it spun me around and then he had it and he was tearing open the paper.

"I tell you that thing just jumped over there and had my lunch before anyone could say scat. Some men were standing around and one of them said he would get it back for me; but by that time the monkey already had his feet in it. He was a large black monkey—about the size of Chris, I'd say—and his feet didn't look at all clean.

"I said to the man, never mind, I didn't believe I wanted it now. The man said he certainly understood. He was as nice as he could be. You know most people are pretty nice when you stop to think about it and I believe he was kind of afraid the monkey would bite him anyway.

"In a minute I got out of there, not hanging around to see if the monkey ate the food or threw it or what. It was a *shock* to me. I knew from going to zoos that if you hand a monkey something he will eat it, but until this morning it never entered my head he would stop you on the street and take it *away* from you."

"My shoes," said Chris. He has no feel for drama which is unrelated to his tight little area of aperception.

She said on this day she had prepared an uncommonly tasty lunch, a ham sandwich, a piece of apple pie and some nice potato salad; and that if the monkey had grabbed the bag the day before it might have choked to death on peanut butter. "But no, do you think that thing would stop me on one of the days I was lunching on knickknacks?"

Downstairs we found a couple of empty chairs in the shoe section and awaited service. Chris had little to say beyond the fact that he desired shoes with a picture of Buster Brown and Brown's dog in them. He removed from his hip pocket a soiled advertisement torn earlier in the week from Kim's copy of *Boy's Life*. The advertisement urged: MAKE A MONSTER! It promises you can build one with your bare hands. PERFECTLY DETAILED DOWN TO THE SMALLEST FANG! DECORATE YOUR ROOM! SURPRISE YOUR MOTHER!

I settle back and wonder vaguely if it would be possible through steady starvation and exercise to reconcile a size-40 waistline with the atrophied buttocks of a pygmy. Chris and I were to return on the following afternoon to alterations and pick up a pair of pants. I had the absurdly optimistic feeling that this was the time I'd secure the ideal fit and Chris would look as neat as Tom Thumb.

The clerk arrived before us in good humor, dropping onto the stool in the graceful sliding squat of the trained seller of shoes. "Something for the little man today?"

Chris glanced up from the monster-kit ad. He is not a coward around adults, only in the company of other children. "I'm not a little man," he said.

There are a half-dozen tryouts of different styles of shoes and Chris does not like them because none bears a picture of Buster Brown and dog. When finally this is made clear and the clerk brings the Buster Browns, Chris selects saddle oxfords with squarish toes and brazen eyelets. He is satisfied with the inner portrait of Brown, even pleased. At one point he even verges on a smile.

Further, the shoes are the necessary inch too long and this is important since his toes grow at a rate almost visible.

The clerk leaves us to change my bill. There is not a speck of color in her face and she does not come up off the stool with the easy speed of a half hour ago. I lean back, eyes closed, reviewing and discarding a series of conciliatory remarks, but am convinced now that whatever I say to the woman it will only make a poor situation worse. I hear Chris rustling around but think little of it.

She returns with the change and it develops that two items are missing, the old pair of shoes (Chris is wearing the new ones) and the box for the new shoes. She stoops and peers beneath our seats and looks under her stool, then moves in wavering circles along the expanse of thick blue carpeting. "This has never happened before," she mutters. "I've seen some funny things in Children's Shoes, but nothing like this." She gazes at Chris, who is either unaware of the inference or doesn't care.

"Did you put the old shoes in the box, honey?" the clerk asked. She looked as if she might at any moment throw back her head and howl.

Chris arose from his chair and paced the carpet on stiff slippery feet, looking hurt and stubborn.

The head of the shoe department was summoned and he ranged over the sector without raising a clue. There was no trace of the box within a radius of twenty feet and Chris offered no self-incriminating evidence, remaining well beyond my reach. The baffling thing was the

§ 260 §

time element. He had simply not had the necessary time to go far—into the basement or upstairs. The search spread throughout the main floor, extending into slacks, costume jewelry and even into leather goods as word passed from department to department. A porter was dispatched to case the alley and he returned, dejected, because it was obvious to him that the assignment was considered important.

Suddenly Chris pointed to the wall behind our clerk, a honey-combed wall of shoes, 10 feet high, perhaps 50 feet long. There were, at irregular intervals, rectangular holes in the wall where new shoes had been removed and sold.

"No," said the clerk. "*No.*"

"Yes ma'am, they're in there somewhere, I stuck the box in a hole in there."

"Ah, *no,*" she whispered. She began loping along the wall of white boxes, flipping off lids. Tissue paper hissed in the boxes and the lids made a clopping sound, rhythmic as a trotting pony, the department manager soon joining her, Chris and I bringing up the rear. Chris seemed really to want to help.

Next day I received a phone call from the clerk and she said they had located the box containing the old shoes. She said she had thought about it most of the night and at last it had struck her that since Chris was only three feet tall the shoes would *have* to be rather near the floor. This was in the nature of a decisive breakthrough in that it eliminated approximately 350 square feet of search area. She said she had gotten onto her knees and moved along the wall, that what she did was to kind of put herself in Chris's place.

She was so delighted at her success she didn't sound the least angry.

I thanked her and told her how sorry I was she had gone to so much trouble. "Just throw them away," I said. "He tells me they hurt his toes." I waited a full minute for her answer, but she said nothing.

Later I called and asked the store to deliver Chris's and my altered pants, explaining that we had changed our minds about the need for another fitting and would not come by as we had planned. It seemed best.

You Look
So Nice
in Your
Gray Suit

MY MOTHER MET US AT THE DOOR AND KISSED US AND
said to Bill, "Son, you look so nice in your gray suit."

Bill was home from Oklahoma for a holiday and he
and I had decided to drive to my mother's for the weekend. She is a terrible cook, my mother is, but Bill and I
figured a couple of days would not hurt us and I wanted
to see her. I have to laugh when people talk about the
way their mothers used to cook this and that and the
other, rolling their eyes and licking their lips. My mother

really sets a firecracker under the dream about mother-cooked food. You can tell from the way she wrestles with it and recoils from it in the raw state that it is not going to be a masterpiece when it comes out of the oven. I would as soon spend a morning in the workroom of a mortuary as to see her stuffing and trussing a turkey.

"You just look *wond*erful," she said to Bill, who is twenty-one and really does look wonderful.

She pulled us into the living room, not saying anything about how I looked. I do not know if this oversight was the result of indifference or if she was just being kind. "Do you smell something burning?" she said to Bill.

He said yes. I said I smelled it, too. It is the smell I remember most clearly from childhood, the smell of scorched food. The next most familiar smell from childhood is that of Hinds Honey & Almond Cream, and after that, ammonia. She used to soak her rings in ammonia in the lavatory. I don't know why she quit doing this or whatever happened to Hinds Honey & Almond Cream. I associate them with pink drying girdles in the bathroom and with Heavenly Hash candy, which she used to bring us from New Orleans when she had been visiting Rachael Miller, whose husband once owned a race horse. My mother never bet on the Miller horse or any other horse and frowns on gambling, drinking and a number of other things. She can smell a drink of whiskey over a long-distance telephone connection. But the smell of burned food doesn't faze her.

Now she says, shrugging, "Ah, well, it must be the cheese toast." Then, to Bill, "I believe you are the best-looking boy I ever saw."

She turns to me, "Don't you think he is the best-looking *thing?*"

"Yes, he is." I go through the dining room and into the kitchen and cut off the oven. I do not bother to look in the oven, because it cannot be anything I haven't seen before. You name it and I have seen her burn it. I have seen her boil away a potful of water and melt the bottom of the pot. You give her a stove and enough time and she can burn asbestos. She is a natural.

When I return to the living room they are seated and we talk for a time about which relatives are drinking too much, or too often, or both. And we discuss briefly the marital bliss or agony of certain relatives, prospects of disaster, and salvation, annoying characteristics, lovable qualities, financial and religious developments. Whenever anything is going wrong for a relative my mother says that what the relative needs is to get closer to God. I have never doubted this and do not doubt it now, but it disconcerts me when she asks me if *I'm* close to God. Assuredly I wish to be, but if there is a reliable yardstick I've never discovered it and sometimes when I am living a most miserably clean life I feel farthest from Him and my prayers bounce back at me from the watermarked ceiling of the bedroom. At other times when I am living more naturally the prayers slide right on through the ceiling into outer space. It is not inevitable that they are received out there, but at least they stand a chance, provided my transmission is not jammed by more powerful or hysterical prayers, which nowadays are probably being sprayed heavenward from every point on the globe.

"You should always wear gray," my mother says to Bill. "Are you saying your prayers in Oklahoma?"

"Yes, ma'am," he says, but I can tell from his face he hasn't prayed in a month, maybe longer. I suspect he quit praying when he went to college, which is when most people discover it is fairly safe and awfully comfortable simply to crawl into bed and go right to sleep.

"That gray *suit*," says my mother, staring in fixed admiration at her grandson. It truly is a nice suit, not expensive but cut well in the Brooks manner, the three-button broken-collarboned look. I am wearing a similar suit but it does not appear to stimulate my mother. I'd rather expected she would take on over me a bit because I'm closer kin than Bill, bone of her bone and all that. At one point she glances at my hands and says they remind her of Louis, my late father, "Those are Louis's hands," she says. This information is conveyed without emphasis and in no way interrupts what, I am convinced, will serve as mainstream of conversation during the weekend.

"I believe Bill's better-looking than Jack," says my mother. "And Jack used to be awfully good-looking."

"Yes." I button and unbutton my jacket and try to relax the muscles of my face. I wonder vaguely about Jack, my cousin. I can never remember if he lives in Shreveport or Dallas. I think he is a geological engineer and knows how things are down under the ground.

"Let me call Sister," my mother says, rising suddenly and going to the phone. "She's dying to see Bill. I know she'll be tickled to death. We'll all drive over to Booboo's Place and eat a Whirliburger. Hello. *Sister?* Hello, this is Sue—you'll never guess who's here! Bill! . . ."

The Art
of Hating
Your Family

YOU OWE IT TO THE MEMBERS OF YOUR FAMILY TO hate them now and then and they owe it to you to hate you a bit.

Hating someone who is kin to you is altogether different than simply hauling off and hating a person you don't care anything about. To hate your family in the manner it deserves to be hated requires careful preparation, sustained conditioning and a degree of discipline.

Let us accept from the beginning that hatred is a wholesome part of family life, as necessary as recreation, penicillin and love. Without hatred there is no contrast and without contrast there is nothing: a sea of syrup and darkling currents of repression which in time may sweep one to the very brink of indifference.

Do not, under any circumstances, seek to hate all the members of your family at one time until you have learned by trial and error how to hate them individually; and it is much better to begin by hating one of the younger children before you tackle the older ones or your wife. Actually, it is easier to hate an older child and you will be tempted in that direction, but older children are narrow-minded in certain areas and are inclined to resent being hated. They are very resourceful in getting back at you and the beginner is not ready for that. By the same token, it is as foolish to start straightaway with your wife as it is to hunt lion with a limber peach-tree switch.

There will be times when you feel you are not making any progress, but keep in mind that nothing worthwhile is accomplished easily. And if you really love your family and wish to remain attuned to it, totally responsive to and aware of it, the least you can do is hate it. I recommend hating a part of it approximately every thirty days, but here there can be no hard-and-fast rule and the situation must be tailored to the requirements of the subject and the material at hand. Some families are more repulsive than others and you must not be discouraged if a friend or acquaintance discloses that he hates every member of his family twenty-four hours a day every day in the year. He is immoderate if not radical and enjoys no more beneficial contrast than if he did not hate at all. Furthermore, they will stand around his bed and laugh when he dies. Nor can you blame them, for it is the old business of too much of a good thing.

In any family of size there is a clear balance of power, and from the standpoint of strategy, which is in the final analysis nothing more than plain common sense, this balance must be taken into consideration by the hater. If I have decided to spend an hour or so hating my wife, I am during that hour especially nice to Jecca, Kim and Chris. If Mary, Jr., happens to be home I buy her a blouse, or at the least a new tube of lipstick. I may write Bill, my oldest son, an encouraging and affectionate letter and allow the other children to read it.

Getting into specifics, let us say that my wife is fixing breakfast and the egg-grease spits on her, which it almost always does. I will say, having carefully attended to the balance of power before saying it, "Could you hurry it a bit, I'm starving."

She will say, "I burned myself."

I will say, "I'm not interested in how you cook yourself, what about the eggs?"

From this point forward her uncontrolled reaction and general venom make it absurdly easy to hate her for the allotted hour. Further, I share the therapy with her, and indications are that on such an occasion she can stand flatfooted and hate circles around me. It is wonderful for her to admit aloud to herself—and to me— what a bastard I am. She has known it for almost a quarter-century and I much longer than that, and it cannot be classified as news or blinding discovery; but how much rosier her cheek and more serene her glance when it is brought out in the open in a familiar atmosphere of overheated Mazola and burned flesh. When the scene is over even her reddish brown bun of hair appears calmer, and domesticer. We feel—in *time,* of course, in *time*—much closer and she is dearer to me than before, for I have once more observed the banked fires of her come to life. Also I have seen her bottom teeth. I am excessively fond of her bottom teeth and she never shows them unless she is angry.

Yet even after you have successfully brought off this kind of thing, you must play it skillfully for the remainder of the day, accepting the fact that a woman does not forget as quickly as a man.

Later, when she asks me what I want for supper, I say without hesitation, "You know, you won't believe it, but I'd like ham steaks and peanut-butter gravy."

She says fine.

I know that she still resents mildly the egg-scene and that ham and peanut-butter gravy is the last thing I may expect for supper. This is perfect because I detest ham and peanut butter.

Hating little children is a snap, but is considerably less rewarding and when you are proficient enough to hate adults with ease you will give it up altogether.

This will not injure the children, this abrupt pinching off of the supply of parental hatred, because all little children hate one another and they get more than their share in the course of a day at school or play. You have heard them at it, "Marjorie, I'm going to kill you if you don't give me the ball." From the standpoint of mental health this impersonal hatred lacks the rich concentrated wallop of family hatred, as we have noted, but little children don't appreciate the importance of specialization and it may be assumed that what their hatred may lack in quality is compensated for by pure quantity and a higher threshold of malevolence.

If you *must* hate a small child now and then and are hard put to establish a reason for doing it (this being a prime obstacle) try hating him for his honesty and youth. I won't guarantee it, but it's better than nothing.

The Egg
and the Ugh

MARY, JR., PEERS AT HER FRIED EGG AND TICKLES THE
white with the tip of her fork. From the mass of the white
she dislodges an acrobatic part of the egg, perhaps the
size of a pea but with a kind of tail on it.

She raises the fork and this thing hangs from it,
trembling. She jiggles the fork and the thing chins itself.
It is neither opaque nor transparent, but a little of both.
Light glimmers around the edges of it.

"Look," she says. "Look at *that.*"

This is a waste of words because all of us are already

looking at it. Her eating techniques have depressed us for years and now that she is in nurses' training her explorations are more fearsome than ever.

With her a meal is not the same as with other people. It is an adventure in vivisection. What she does with an egg is *nothing*.

She really comes into her own with a T-bone steak. The way she takes it apart is something to see. I have always been of the opinion such an operation is wasted at table in front of a group of laymen. Using the knife in slick curving strokes, she first removes the rim of fat from around the meat. As she makes the initial cut she is cautious but as soon as the incision is started she becomes a different person. Gone is the wariness. There is no slightest sign of timidity.

Nor should there be, for this slip of a girl has performed the steakotomy at least a thousand times. She has done it on a shaky card table in the backyard in the shadow of the barbecue grill with night bugs hurling themselves at her head. She has performed it in dimly lit restaurants outside Gulfport and Biloxi with gin-crazed tourists knocking against her elbows.

When the fat is cleared she lifts it free and since there is no need for hemostat or siphon she sweeps without pause into the more critical phase of extracting the bone. When it is done she deposits it in the center of her salad and it lies there. Alongside it on the bed of lettuce is the fat, looking somehow tireder and more extracted than the bone.

A streak of roasted gristle is next. It offers resistance of a nature to make the blood run thin; but her face is expressionless. My wife has left the table some time ago and Jecca now pushes back her chair and tries to smile, bunching green cheeks.

Even Kim shows signs of deterioration, eating more and more slowly. He has begun chewing his food, a sure sign of nervousness. When he is up to taw he swallows things whole after simply biting them once or twice to let them know who is boss.

Chris is disinterested; but I don't feel at all well. I know from past experience I will be able to stick it, yet it is not a heartwarming prospect.

After all, you don't *have* to watch what Mary, Jr., is doing. I don't know why I look at it at *all*, but there is something about the operation that pulls at the eyeballs, like carelessly arranged pictures in a stereo holder, so that finally when it comes into focus and the scattered images fuse in depth, the reality of the torn steak on the plate is almost too much for the mind to absorb. It seems impossible that this steak, five hours earlier, rested comfortably in a case at the Atlantic & Pacific Tea Company.

Actually, Mary, Jr., has no desire to be a surgeon and truly intends to become a registered nurse. But ever since I can remember she has been afraid that some day she will swallow a piece of fat or a knob of gristle. She has no fear of bones and removes them only because she believes they may camouflage fat or gristle.

She has a fixation about eating veins, too. And although this is no place for a graphic description of the performance, I have seen her vein the leg of a broiled chicken in a manner that is suffocatingly skillful. That is all I shall say about it.

In the matter of conveying food to her mouth once she has dismembered it, Mary, Jr., is the picture of daintiness. She neither dawdles nor gobbles and I have no fault to find in this quarter, where so many of us, young and old alike, fall short.

As for the eggectomy, it has no real place here, in that it requires nothing beyond piercing curiosity and eyesight, and I feel the mention of it is like bringing up hangnails at the scene of an air crash..

It has nonetheless impressed me, because I used to be so innocent about eggs and believed there were only two parts to them. Three, counting the shell. Oh, I knew that once in a great while you might encounter a freak with two yolks, but it never occurred to me there could be anything hidden. Now I find myself looking for the secretive, springy blip in my own egg and herding it off to the edge of the plate. Once or twice I have de-fatted a small chop, just to see if I could do it. There are, I will admit, moments when I consider moving on to bigger experiments, but I have neither the nerve nor the training for it. One can't with any hope of success begin these things so late in life.

That
of the Parsley

"IT NEEDS PARSLEY," I SAY, LIFTING THE DIMPLED aluminum pot lid and breathing deeply. "It's the parsley that makes the soup."

"No," Mary says. "I'm what makes the soup."

I return the lid to the pot. "Well, you don't have to get ugly about it."

She is chopping green things on the redwood table. She uses the knife more feelingly than seems necessary.

§ 277 §

"You're always sounding off about parsley. To hear you tell it the parsley comes in the kitchen and stands over the stove and works like a dog."

I say, "Well, you have to admit parsley kind of brings out the taste."

"I'm sick to my teeth of hearing about parsley." She chops harder and faster, the blade almost blurred. "Every time I cook you come in here and start dithering about how your mother or your Aunt Clara used parsley. My God, they must've put the stuff in the toothpaste."

"—now wait a minute."

"No, *you* wait a minute. I've listened to all I can take. Last week when I was broiling the chicken you prissed in here braying about parsley. It was the same with the potatoes. Parsley's what makes potatoes good, you said. I'm fed to here with it. I work for hours to get a decent dinner ready and you tell me it's parsley that makes it good. Please," she says. "Go watch TV, go write a best-seller, *anything.*"

"I'm tired of writing," I say. "I can't get the people to move around and do anything, they just sit in chairs and think cheap, involved thoughts. They don't even go to bed—with each other, I mean." I lean against the table. Even with the lid on the pot you can smell the soup cooking. The hot-water heater goes plup-plup-plup, a good calm sound, like rocks falling in mud. "There's nothing to get so excited about," I say, knowing that it will irritate her further because if there is a single thing she despises being told more than any other, it is this.

She continues chopping the green stuff. "The first five years we were married it was onions. You said it was onions that made everything good. I went around stinking to high heaven. Sundays in church I could smell myself when I lifted my hands to take the collection plate. Then it was bay leaves. And celery. You had me jamming so much celery in the oyster stew I couldn't stick the ladle in the pot to serve it."

"I was only trying to help."

"I want to go on record once and forevermore as stating that when anything you eat in this house is good, *I'm* what makes it good." She turns abruptly and looks at me with a complete absence of expression. "I am the cook and I have always been the cook, except when I was in the hospital having babies, or getting ready to have them or getting over having them."

This is pretty much the truth. In the years of our marriage she has read a few detective stories and played a bit of bridge, mind you; it hasn't been all culinary or obstetrical, but her song of resentment now, though I consider it to be both bloated and acrobatic in content, is a fairly honest tune.

I say nothing of the dozens of eggs I have fried on Sunday nights or other chores rendered as assistant mother and short-order cook. It is apparent that she is crazed with self-pity and there is no need to add to the inflammation.

She says: "You came in here Thanksgiving and said it was the basting that made the turkey good—baste it, you said. That's all there is to it, that's the secret."

"I'm sorry." I pat her and she withdraws from the caress. "What's that you're chopping?"

She wipes the knife and lays it on the board, little

beetles of light crawling along the blade. She seizes a double handful of cut greens, bright and frizzly things, dumping them into the soup. "It's parsley," she says. "And don't you open your mouth."

Some
Bracelets
Have
Arthritis

I FEEL RELIEVED BECAUSE IT IS STILL TWO WEEKS UNTIL
Christmas and already I've bought my wife's Christmas
present and have shown it to her and taken it back to the
store and told them she doesn't want it. Usually it is the
very day before Christmas that the store learns it must
refund the money. This makes for ugly feeling all around
and you can't blame the store either, because it seems no
matter what I select for Mary it isn't quite right. One year
I bought her just about the nicest and most unusual gift
available, a small slab of polished petrified wood from

Germany with a rounded hole for sticking your thumb into when you desired to rub it. The clerk said it was a touchstone of the first class and that regardless of which thumb you used in the rubbing, that rounded hole was the ideal fit.

Anyway, this year I started early.

Throughout the years I have learned my lesson well; and now when I gird my wallet and set forth on the jostling seas of commerce there is no foolish hope in my breast, no distorting haze of sentiment, for I am secure in the knowledge that the initial purchase of a present is only the first leg of what may be a many-legged journey. This is no absurdly simple proposition like buying Kim a leather punch kit that will go all the way through the heel of his hand on first try. The gift for Mary must be expensive enough so that she will prefer almost immediately the idea of the cash, saving me a series of return trips to swap presents, none of which will be any more satisfactory than the first; and at the same time the gift must not be so costly that it will set an insane precedent, placing me in the strained position of trying to top it the following year. It entails more than a careless feel for anticipated revenue. Further, the Christmas present must under no circumstances be one which, although it qualifies for rapid rejection, nonetheless excites Mary's appetite for a similar gift. This was the case three years ago with a suede jacket, which aroused her interest in a full-length coat of glazed crimson leather, which, in turn, focused her seasonal greed on an alligator handbag not quite the size of an MG convertible. The logical progression, when I had bought and returned all of these (except the MG) was for her to select for herself a black four-door Rambler. And this she did, explaining that it would save enough on gasoline to pay for itself, an angle I continue to roll dully around in my mind. I know there is a flaw in it somewhere, but can't put my finger on it.

At any rate, and the rates are hell in the stores this time of year, I now select carefully a clerk who is small-boned and unaggressive, so that when I return with the loot there will be no harrowing scene.

In truth I've never become completely adjusted to the tight, suffering smile of even the tiniest clerk, but such grimaces are easier on nerve and tissue than a plain out-and-out dogfight.

This year I bought Mary a golden bracelet of a seething design, the links forming a kind of ventilated rope. I mean it was round but you could see through it. There is a better way to describe it but I've forgotten what it said in the pamphlet. This was a pedigreed bracelet, with papers in the box, these papers explaining that the bracelet wasn't something whomped up overnight, that it was the final result of a series of magnificent advances which had transpired in the jewelry trade over a period of centuries. No fooling. Cellini and all that. Italy, Spain, sultry breezes, even a hint of sexuality. A love-inspired bracelet, limber as a goose, snakelike.

For a silly instant I half-believed Mary might keep it.

A man and his wife were standing next to me and he was buying her a camera because they had no picture of their Pomeranian; she said they never wanted to forget how the dog looked when it was young and untroubled. The woman said she thought the bracelet stunning and that it was exactly what she would like for Christmas if she didn't need a camera but that Pomeranians are young

only a few weeks and if you don't photograph them in a hurry you've had it.

She added that the golden bracelet was about the limberest she'd ever seen and the clerk said, beaming, that that was one of the finest things about it, because it would twist this way and that and catch whatever light there was. On the grayest, rainiest day it would writhe around until it picked up a ray.

I had him gift-wrap it, which is a senseless but integral part of the game, as important in its way as Mary's own responsibility of rejection. In rejecting the gift she must follow the time-worn rule of discovering a legitimate reason for her action and this is not always easy. She had the devil of a time explaining what was wrong with that German rock with the thumb-hollow in it. I don't recall exactly how she engineered that one, but it had something to do with her hands sweating, especially the balls of her thumbs.

Even though Christmas was distant I carried the bracelet home and handed it to Mary. Early delivery has become an accepted part of the rite. Along with ritualistic dialogue.

"I've bought your present."

"What *is* it?"

"I just want you to feel the package, you'll have to wait until Christmas."

"No, let me see it *now*."

"Oh, all right then, go ahead—just a peek."

You know how it goes.

Well, sir, you won't believe it but somewhere en route home that snake of a bracelet developed arthritis of the worst kind. When I'd clasped it on her wrist she gasped at the beauty of it, then called my attention to a stiff hump near one end of it. No amount of massage or manipulation served to eliminate the golden hump. She tried to appear pleased. "I just love it," she said, rubbing at the hump. She had turned in a wonderfully elegant performance and I felt quite proud of her.

This morning I took it back to the man, who has been through this with me on other occasions. I laid the narrow box on the glass counter and he stood there a moment, hands spread flat along the glass, asking no questions, whistling quietly between his teeth. Finally he said without looking up, "You want to try and find something else, maybe?"

"No," I said. "I'm giving her the money."

He looked up then and smiled. There were tears of gratitude in his kindly brown eyes.

Sports
Car

WE HAD DRIVEN FROM THE CAR LOT TO THE RESTAU-
rant in the white car and now as I chewed shrimp, enjoying the sting of horseradish in my nose, I could look out
a large window of plate glass and see the car only a few
yards from our table. The red leather insides of the
roadster glimmered and you could almost smell the
fresh leather through the plate glass. I am a sucker for
red leather, you could line the inside of a leprosarium
with red leather and I would want to buy it if the payments were halfway reasonable.

§ 287 §

"It's a lot-of-fun car," said the redheaded man who was trying to sell me on the idea of the sports car. "What the hell, you and me, we aren't getting any younger."

I guess he meant that in a few years I would be too stiff to crawl in and out of a fun-car; because even now it was not easy and could not be done in haste. Earlier I had sat on a steel corner of the doorpost instead of the seat and although I'd said nothing and neither did he, he must have known it hurt. "She will get zero to sixty in seven or eight seconds," said the redheaded man. "You can take off the top and breathe God's good sunshine and air, it's the difference between captivity and *freedom*."

I ate shrimp and drank ice-cold beer. "I hadn't thought of it that way," I said, feeling fevered and nervous.

"You ought to go ahead and get it," the man said, taking a bite of his fried chicken and watching me. "You *owe* it to yourself."

He added: "We'll give top dollar on a trade."

I stared at the car. "I don't think so, my wife won't be happy about a trade and my friends will say I've gone into second puberty."

"You should be so lucky," said the redheaded man, prying loose another chunk of white meat.

"No," I said, "I've only made three payments on my Buick, it's like new except for a couple of cough-drop stains."

"Cough drop?"

"Yes," I said, not explaining.

He laughed. "Well, you're the doctor."

He seemed to have an appropriate answer for everything.

The last thing in the world I'd intended was to stop

here in Chattanooga on the way home. I saw the white car on my way to Asheville to do a piece on a salty little judge and it was nice and warm as I whizzed past in the Buick and I told myself I was lucky to be inside such a warm, smooth car and not in the little white car which probably made farting noises from the exhaust and wouldn't start on a cold day. It was an English car and once I owned an old Jag Mark VII Saloon that had to be pushed off in the morning because it was so cold-natured, yet if you got caught in traffic it overheated so that steam practically came out of your ears. Mary told me at the time that if I ever bought another "hunk of foreign junk" there would be the hell of a scene and possibly a separation. She has a great deal of common sense in some areas and I respect it, but coming back through Chattanooga I stopped at the car lot just for laughs and to confirm the fact that I was lucky to own the Buick with power steering and V-8 engine and all that. After all, you can't beat Detroit when it comes to turning out power and comfort.

The redheaded man had come out and he was very friendly and the least I could do was climb under the wheel of the white car and go farting down the road a piece with him. It was sprung stiff in the manner of all racing cars and you counted the bumps in the road with the tip of your spine. There were four speeds forward and every time you slowed down you had to shift gears and work the clutch pedal like a church organist. On top of that the wind in the cloth top went bop-bop-bop and the transmission moaned like it was going to break down in tears.

"What you think of it?" the redheaded man said.

"It's comical," I said.

§ *290* §

It was a brand new car, with only thirteen miles on it, but it rattled all over. We passed a rough stretch where they were patching the highway and it sounded like a blacksmith shop falling down an elevator shaft.

"What's that?" I said.

He lit a cigarette. "It's characteristic, it's characteristic of these cars, they're built to go in, not to sleep in."

I said, "My Buick would go by this thing so fast it would suck it right up the exhaust."

"You're dreaming," he said. "I tell you what, you wait till we get clear up here and you stomp down on her, really kick her in the pants."

A small button of red glass glowed on the dashboard. The redheaded man said that some kind of a minor adjustment was needed in the voltage regulator, or maybe the generator should be inspected. "We can fix that, you go ahead and kick her in the britches."

I kicked her.

He said, "Is it still comical?"

"No," I said, my mouth feeling dry.

"Let's stop down here and get us some lunch," the man said. "You can't do business on an empty stomach."

Inside the office at the car lot after lunch there were several men sitting around looking half-angry and half-happy, the way car salesmen do. They grinned angrily and got up and went outside so that we would have more room. The redheaded man fished a pad of printed forms out of a desk and the old familiar trapped feeling stole over me. You feel weak and lost when they get you sitting in a chair looking at all the papers and the light shining on the barrel of the ballpoint pen while they write numbers, adding, subtracting, scratching out.

I jumped up. "No," I said. "No, I've been a jackass all my life. Once in Denver I bought a new Ford and I kept trading until I didn't have any car at all."

The redheaded man shrugged. "Okay, you're the *judge.*"

"You know as well as I that I'll look like a damned fool going home in that thing. My God, next thing you know I'd be sashaying around in one of those squashed plaid caps."

Outside I could see the Buick sedan and next to it the loudmouthed white car.

I said, "How much are the payments?"

I arrived home smelling of shrimp and sunshine and gasoline fumes and Mary took a look at the car and went into the kitchen. She did not even ask what I'd done with the Buick. I asked her if she would like a drink and there was none of the usual hesitation, she said yes she believed she would like a real one. While we drank at the redwood table in the kitchen I read the manual, which is put out by the makers of the car. The first page disturbed me. It said to use pure rainwater when replenishing the water in the radiator; that plain water would cause "*a deposit on the inner surfaces of the cooling system, thus reducing efficiency.*"

"You look pale," Mary said. "It must have been a hard drive in that thing."

"It was fine," I said. I asked her if it had rained any while I was gone. She said no it hadn't, that this always was the dry time of year and it might go a month without a drop. She said once it went ten weeks.

"Well," I said, "it better rain soon."

§ 292 §

She said: "Don't tell me you bought a farm, too; what did you trade for that—the house? The *children*?"

It was the last word she said to me between then and now.

Surely it will rain soon. Last evening there were some fat black clouds in the east and I jumped in the car and drove for an hour in that direction but nothing happened. I may have to go over to New Orleans and wait there. It rains just about all the time in New Orleans.

You'll
Be Home
in an Hour

MY WIFE SAID THAT IF THE TOOTH WAS BOTHERING me it was silly not to go on down to the dentist and be done with it, that I'd be home in an hour. When it comes time for me to go to the dentist she is the bravest person in the world and to hear her talk you would think there was no more joyous occasion than the installation of a series of gumline fillings or the removal of a mutinous molar. She is not nearly so swift or cheerful in dealing with her own teeth. I do not say she declines altogether

§ 294 §

to cope with her own, only that she does it with less exhilaration.

"Just think," she says. "If you go now you'll be home before noon and all of it will be *behind* you."

I stall for time, reading a Hattie Carnegie advertisement in an old Harper's Bazaar, a magazine which never fails to amaze me. In the ad Hattie relates a commonplace, homely little workaday incident: a customer desires a new dress that will show off her diamond necklace but she doesn't want to take the diamonds out of the vault at this time. ". . . It was thus that on that sunny morning we retired with the dress and the fitter to the bank vault where we held the fitting. The woman retired gracefully and reappeared, to the guards' astonishment, in her evening dress. We measured the length of the necklace, we fitted the dress to play up the gems; and we secretly wished for Alec Guinness, who would have stolen the necklace, rushed off for Idlewild and thence to South America. It was an idle dream and we went back to work. . . ."

My wife is sweeping the porch. She wears a tuna-colored sweater and jeans and loafers that are coming unsewed. I try to imagine her in the vault of the Citizens Bank, where we usually are overdrawn. I touch the ailing tooth with my tongue, then slide the tip of the tongue along the gum where the needle will be plunged. I close my eyes.

"What's the *matter?*" Mary says.

"The needle. I don't mind the other, it's the way your lip dies on one side."

"Oh, *that.*" She sweeps in good spirit, not sweeping the dust out the door, but up into the air, so that some of it floats out through the screen but most of it hangs flat in the sunlight.

I read another ad in another woman-type magazine. This one says Millicent loves wool, she craves wool, she has to have wool.

The whole ad is devoted to the proposition that if Millicent is ever deprived of wool she will be in the hell of a mess and will probably die naked and deranged. There is a picture of a woman in a bright wool dress. I guess it is Millicent. She looks pleased and judging from her smile she never has to go to the dentist. I reflect that if I had Millicent's teeth I wouldn't worry about anything at all and I most certainly would not act silly over wool, because some of the synthetics are quite warm and attractive. It says so on the next page.

"They can make fur out of chemicals," I say to my wife, who stands knee deep in layers of dust.

"Go on," she says. "Go on down town, honest, sometimes you are a terrible baby."

"I'll phone first."

"Well, phone, do it now."

The dentist's assistant says no, there will be no need to wait, the doctor can take me right now; that for the first time in weeks no one is waiting in the anteroom. "You hit it just right," she says. She is smiling, I can tell. The smile squashes the words.

There is something bad about going into a dentist's office and marching straight to the chair without even a final cigaret. The transition is too abrupt. You do not have time to gather the fear into a hard little lump under your wishbone and since the fear is not encysted it flows from scalp to toenails, whirling thinly like the water in the porcelain bowl you spit in. I stare into the bowl while the napkin is tied under my chin. The bowl is clean but already I can see the twisted strings of blood going down the hole. The hole makes hungry noises and the dentist asks what I think about Wisconsin knocking off Northwestern, the No. 1 team in the nation.

I look at my watch. It is 9:30 A.M. The crystal is sweating from inside so that there are beads of water under the glass. A few minutes ago I was safe at home. Outside the sun is shining and people are walking around laughing. The first needle is very long and seems to pump up the right side of my head. "I'd never've thought Wisconsin would bump Northwestern," says the dentist.

I spit into the bowl after the second needle. The assistant hands him the needles and helps peer into my mouth. She has a nice way of looking into a mouth and you get the feeling, watching her face, that it must look pretty good in there. She is young, pregnant, and her brown hair shines. You can tell she doesn't have a chicken bone in her body and that she is not *about* to run out of needles.

By 10:30 A.M. the tooth is out but there is the matter of the tip of the root, which is hooked over the bone somewhere under the floor of the sinus. By now there have been so many needles it doesn't matter a great deal to me, this complication. Let them laugh outside in the sunshine, let them chew gum and tell jokes. My brave, inflated head is dead. I am but an observer. Here in the dentist's office we have become a smoothly functioning team. My head is the ball. The dentist is Wisconsin. Whenever the pain threatens to return he pumps up the ball with another needle. At 1:30 P.M. he informs me he

has lost the tip of the root of the tooth; that it now lies in the sinus and will require the attention of a dental surgeon.

"There is a man in New Orleans," say the dentist. "He's the best. I'll phone him and you can hop right on over there. If I were you, *I'd* want him."

He makes the appointment for me and stuffs something in my cheek and I get on a bus and go to New Orleans. I do not stop by the house to see my wife. I am not angry with her, only indifferent. On the bus to New Orleans I wonder vaguely why it is that Millicent has got to have wool.

It is well into the night when the dental surgeon is through with me and I am sitting waiting for the bus to come. My right eye is closed to a slit. I can see only the middle of people through the slit when I shut the good eye. I have not eaten since breakfast. There is a fellow sitting next to me and he is eating what appears to be a chicken-fried baby, removing the parts from a brown paper bag that is dark with grease. He eats with an exaggerated movement of the jaw, not a straight champing, but a rotation of the kind you associate with singers like Tommy Sands or whoever it was that married Sinatra's daughter.

He catches my glance and holds out the bag to me. "Squirrel," he says. "Squirrel and rabbit."

I shake my head. I am glad he is not eating somebody's child but I wish he would go away because I am too weak to get up. It has taken all my strength to make the phone call to my wife from the booth at the bus station; and the talk with her was less than satisfactory. She could not

§ *299* §

understand my blubbering and she kept saying she was worried sick. She said she just knew I'd be home in an hour or two and she couldn't believe it when she phoned the dentist and he said I was in New Orleans.

"You better eat some a this," the man says, shaking the paper sack. "It will do you good and help you, *too*, ha-ha-ha-, I *know*. I use to be bad about drinkin' and fightin' myself. I was on the bum a year. Use to wait 'til it rained and I would go stand outside a supermarket until a lady got in her car with her groceries. There she would be all warm and snug in her car with food packed all 'round her and I would take off my hat, the rain bouncing off my skull, and I'd say Miss, can you spare me a *dime?*"

I close my good eye and observe his middle through the slit. There is rabbit grease or something on the stomach of his shirt. It makes my head ring. I hope he is not going on the northbound bus. I do not believe I can stand to be shut up in a bus with him and his bag. "I use to drink paint-thinner," he continues. "Paint-thinner will make you climb the wall. Once I laid down in a ditch outside Natchez and tried to die, but the weeds tickled my nose and I had to get up."

They are calling my bus now. I stand up carefully and the man keeps his seat. It is my first decent break of the day. Walking to the bus I am afraid to look back but it is all right, my luck truly seems to have changed and I will be home by morning. Like Mary said, all of it will be behind me.

How
to Get Along
with
Your Family
Though Drunk

PERHAPS NO ACCOUNT OF AMERICAN FAMILY LIFE, NO matter how loosely woven, and we have set some kind of record for loose weaving here, is complete without at least a cursory inspection of the drinking problem. If it can be considered a problem. From earliest youth I have considered drinking a luxury, but this callow approach is no longer in fashion, or even tolerable. It is, for one thing, in direct conflict with the popular concept of The Dignity of Mankind, a national craze discussed earlier.

My theory about drinking is that if you are not going

to get at least slightly drunk what is the use of fouling up your breath and wasting the money? Yet I have scant patience with falling-down drunks, or even stumbling drunks, or the ones who like to phone long-distance around midnight (inevitably calling a place where it is two o'clock in the morning). In my earnest opinion this latter group is more obnoxious than all the belligerents, erotics, and fallers-down combined, and the problem will not be eliminated until a system of issuing telephone licenses is devised and perfected. To qualify for a telephone license the applicant would have to drink two Kraft cheese glasses full of straight Cutty Sark at midnight and sit within easy reach of a telephone for a full hour without placing a single call, either local or long-distance.

About the Kraft cheese glasses.

I have been measuring whiskey into them in the kitchen for so long that I am lost without a Kraft cheese glass and cannot accurately judge my condition with any other unit of measure. I do not know how many standard shots may be divided into a Kraft cheese glass, but I do know that three of the glasses (each three-quarters filled) makes me feel fine; and four of them comprise a mistake of major proportions.

After the first glassful I feel a pleasant stinging high in my nose and the kitchen begins to look somehow more valuable and attractive. Even the washing machine develops a certain charm and the handle of the refrigerator becomes both an object of art and an engineering masterpiece. I admire its cleverly concealed little spring and the smooth chromed length of the handle, the pure vertical line silken and unabashed in the dying sunlight.

§ 302 §

I go out into the backyard and look at the car and the dent in the left-front fender is not so deep as I had thought. The car has an air of crouching power and I am inclined to discard the cynical knowledge that the motor has crouched to such an extent it requires new supports.

The grass around me seems healthier than I had remembered and I wave and pucker my nose in a friendly manner when I see my neighbor in her yard, squatting studiously in plaid shorts, punching at the ground with some kind of tool. I do not resent the fact that when she sweeps the driveway out front between the two houses she clears the pine needles only from her half. After all, she is a busy woman and it does not really matter that the needles fall from her tree. I stroll out front. It is a beautiful tree, what they used to call a virgin pine before they understood the dark facts of pollenization.

Back in the kitchen I swallow my second belt of Cutty Sark and study the black sailing ship on the label. My nose no longer stings but there is the continued and heightened feeling that we live among beautiful things. A single droplet of water hangs from the faucet of the sink, stretching and contracting, now and again tucking in its rounded little silver behind, as if afraid to make the plunge. In this single truth-laden instant, this quivering moment in eternity, it has achieved identity as a droplet. It is an individual and dreads return to the anonymous molecules, the seething and unseen movements of the waters of the world.

Mary comes into the kitchen and I mix her a Scotch and water, with plenty of ice, using a tall glass. "Don't overdo it," she says automatically.

I am pained but say nothing.

Mary, Jr., is home for the weekend and she lies stiffly on her bed in the room off the kitchen. She is wheezing and looking at the light fixture which hangs over her bed. She frequently develops asthma when we drink and ordinarily when she is home I stick to milk, water and iced tea. "What's the matter?" I ask, knowing.

She coughs and sits up, holding her chest. "Oh, nothing—do you know where Mama put my spray?"

The spray is in the refrigerator. It is in a little gray plastic bag which is quite cold and depressing to handle. I take it to her and she sits up and cocks her jaws apart and squeezes the bulb on the spray, sucking in the cold mist, not looking at me. She looks strangled and doomed. I have never done anything mean to her when I was drinking; in fact I often give her money, trying to buy some kind of reprieve. There are other things besides the drinking that make her wheeze and for this I am thankful. When she gets around her grandmothers she needs the spray, although neither of the grandmothers drinks and my own mother goes to church every Sunday. Not being able to buy a sweater or skirt she desires sometimes makes Mary, Jr., come down with an attack too, but these are easily cured. All you have to do is get in the car and take her downtown and buy the sweater or skirt. You don't even have to like the color or fit of them. Recovery is total and practically instantaneous and it is cheaper than paying for a new series of allergy tests or a Chihuahua.

She has a ravening appetite for clothing and when she runs long limber fingers over a piece of material in a department store, the cloth seems to come alive beneath her hands, to writhe with reflex affection. Her hands are built narrow and smooth, like the rest of her, and they are incredibly swift and accurate at the business of handling the fastenings of freshly bought clothing; she can button up behind herself from coccyx to nape of neck in a few sparse and fluid movements. No matter what she puts on it looks smart and as if it cost more than a dress should. Often it has. Clothing is to her what chocolate is to Jecca, what sports and the outdoors are to Kim, what running from a good fight is to Chris.

Now I say to her as she plops the spray in its cold bag: "Why don't you go downtown and shop awhile?" I hear my wife's ice clinking in the kitchen.

The third Kraft cheese glassful does not restore my mood, but it achieves certain minor repairs of spirit. My wife has gone into the front of the house to dig around under all the Stravinsky and Tchaikovsky in quest of Brubeck. Chris and Jecca enter in sudden acute need for ice water. They spend so much time with each other that their movements are curiously synchronized and when they come into a room it is as if they are hooked together, shoulder-to-kidney, traveling at the same pace but at different levels. They make much noise with the ice water and when they are finished both look up at me at once. Even their water drinking is geared to mutuality, to a common swallow, an identical thirst. Frequently they hate each other, but no one can deny they are attuned, almost to the degree of freakishness.

"What's *that?*" they say.

I used to tell them it was "grownup ginger ale." Now I sit on the edge of the sink, my buzz wilting within me. "It's whiskey."

"Whis-key," Jecca says to Chris.

§ *305* §

Then, to me, "It sure is a pretty bottle, I bet it cost plenty."

I inhale deeply ."Thanks, I'm glad you like my bottle."

"It's Scotch, isn't it?"

"Yes."

"Cutty Sark."

"Yes, it's Cutty Sark."

Chris sticks out his tongue and looks crosseyed at the tip of it. "Cutty Sark," he says. "Old Cutty Sark."

"They are starting a new class for beginners at dancing school," says Jecca. "I could begin next week and it doesn't cost but a little." She gazes pensively at my cheese glass, too subtle to stare directly at the costly bottle of Cutty Sark. Her timing in matters of this nature is almost professionally good and her oily eyelids, periodically lowered and raised, lend high drama to her projects. There is a stealthy, semaphoric quality to the light which bounces from the lids.

"All right," I say.

"I think it's just a few dollars a month."

"Fine, why don't you walk down to Mrs. Gladney's and talk it over with her, the price and everything—and take Chris along with you."

"Thank you, Daddy." Lids glistening. She does a twist and Chris joins her, their rumps swinging in unison, his smaller and closer to the floor. "Hot damn," he says. "Hot damn."

Jecca, grinning, cuffs him and seizes his arm, "You talk like that and you can't go with me, you *hear*?"

"Old Cutty Sark," says Chris as he is pulled from the room.

I fill the fourth glass three-quarters to the top and I

know it is a bad thing to do, but, as the saying goes, you can't fly on one feather and now that all the children are bought and gone, I may as well try briefly for the mountaintop. The Cutty Sark slides down in the civilized manner for which it is famous and its gentle coals warm my wishbone, the warmth spreading and expanding to the tip of the liver and showering into the stomach. Like I say, drinking is more a luxury than a problem. But it is a luxury I am beginning to believe I can scarce afford.